TEN SECRETS
For Achieving A Successful
Celestial Marriage

By Laura Nielson Denke

Published by
AMERICAN PRESS SERVICES, INC.
2247 15th Avenue West, Seattle, WA 98119

Printed in the United States of America

1st printing, 1999

Library of Congress Catalog Card Number: 99-95422

ISBN: 9673865-0-0

Jacket and book design by Sherri Scott

Layout and page design by Gina Griffin Hanzsek, Griffin Graphics

Final edit by Sharleen and Creede Lambard

Dedicated to
Conrad W. Denke, my True Love.

PUBLISHER'S NOTE

Although the concepts presented in Ten Secrets for Achieving a Successful Celestial Marriage can be of great benefit, some couples may require marriage counseling and/or other kinds of help. Marriage counseling can be arranged through LDS Social Services and through other professionals who offer these valuable services. Also, spouses who suffer abuse can seek safety and counsel through city, county, and state agencies.

This book is not intended for the treatment of psychiatric disorders. Those who may be suffering from depression and other mood disorders, anxiety disorders, or other psychiatric disorders can seek professional consultation from licensed professionals such as psychiatrists, physicians, and psychologists.

This book is a reflection of the author's experiences and not an official statement of LDS church doctrine.

Names and certain details of many of the stories cited in this book have been changed to protect the anonymity of the people involved.

FOREWORD

Perspective is the ability to judge the relative importance of an event in the context of its time and place in history. During World War II, my father was involved in two major naval battles which determined the course of the war. One was the Battle of Midway and the other was the Battle of the Coral Sea. I asked my father to describe these two significant, historic encounters and his answer disappointed me. "It was just a bunch of noise," he said. "Noise," I said, "bombs dropping, planes crashing, battleships sinking and that's all you remember?" "No," he smiled, "when the war was over I got a book and read about it."

Marriage and raising a family is often "just a bunch of noise." Unless the couple involved is able to maintain an "eternal perspective," they risk losing more than a battle and more than a war. They risk the loss of an eternal family.

Ten Secrets for Achieving a Successful Celestial Marriage is a practical guide which will help any marriage maintain the eternal perspective.

Thirty-two years as a marriage and family counselor have convinced me that the principles Laura writes about in this work will strengthen any marriage. I commend her for her efforts and recommend, without reservation, this book to all who are seeking for a Celestial Relationship.

Dr. John L. Lund

*"Partners in a celestial marriage
always seek to see one another
through God's all knowing eyes."*

TABLE OF CONTENTS

Five Pillars of a
Celestial Marriage

Nightly Couple's Prayer

Daily Talk Time

Weekly Date

Weekly Planning Session

Scripture Study

CHAPTER 1

THE FIVE PILLARS OF
A CELESTIAL MARRIAGE

That morning the brooding Seattle sky was ominous. Undaunted, I strapped my toddler into her stroller, put up my red umbrella and jogged down the pavement at a steady clip. Passing a plethora of forsythia and lilac in bloom, I drew in a breath of sweet fragrances. Elisabeth clapped her hands together, jolting me out of my 'Walter Mitty-like' state of mind, and pointed to the brick Tudor house partially camouflaged by blooming rhododendron bushes. Whether my daughter saw Sarah in the window, or the Spirit was working through her, I know that when I glanced at the oak carved door of Sarah's residence, I felt impressed to approach and ring her doorbell.

Sarah's long brown tresses covered her tear stained face as she opened the door and motioned for me to enter. I put my arm around her delicate shoulders and squeezed her gently. Tugging at the strands of her hair as if they were unwanted weeds, she flipped them behind her ears revealing a forced smile. I placed Elisabeth on the floor next to Lily, where the two of them began playing with a set of alphabet blocks. Sarah choked on her words, intermingled with audible cries. Just then a torrent of rain burst from the sky beating against the leaded glass windowpanes. For the past year Sarah and Jake had been fighting. She was devastated. She couldn't confide in her mother who was in the midst of a divorce. Her father was deceased, and her friends' marriages were worse off than hers.

One by one, her problems tumbled from her trembling lips. At last, weary from expressing her emotions, she leaned back on the faded and cracked burgundy leather couch and closed her eyes. "I suppose you think that I'm terrible?" She queried.

"Hardly," I laughed, "I'm far from perfect myself. Besides, all of your problems can be solved."

"They can?" she asked incredulously.

"Sure... with work." I assured her.

"Can you help me? Save my marriage? I mean..." Sarah whimpered through her splayed hands.

"Definitely. In fact I've helped quite a few couples who've been in situations similar to yours. I know I can help you. And I'd like to help you, but..."

"But what?" She asked interrupting nervously.

"It takes a lot of work."

"I can do work."

"Well, I can't help you, unless..."

"Unless what?" She asked anxiously.

"Unless you and your husband do the assignments I will give you."

Sarah grimaced. "Arg..." She grunted. "Can't you just tell us what we are doing wrong."

"I could. For that matter many people could tell you what is wrong in your marriage. I'm sure you and your husband probably can too!"

"No kidding," Sarah remarked sarcastically.

"Far more important than learning what is wrong in your marriage is learning the principles that you must live in order to obtain a celestial marriage. Living these principles is what will make the difference in your marriage and create the changes you so desperately need."

"I can't possibly commit my husband to do any assignments, and I don't have time to do them. I'm already too busy with my life. You know, the children, school, PTA, church, my calling, volunteer work..." Sarah's words trailed off.

"It's up to you. You are the one who has to decide what is a priority in your life. Listen, I don't want to waste any more of your time."

I stood up from the burgundy couch and heard the maple hardwood floorboards creak beneath my footfalls as I edged towards the toddlers at play. I scooped up Elisabeth in my arms and strapped her into the stroller. I pivoted the stroller on its wheels and paused before making my exit.

"I just want you to remember that principles of a celestial marriage are only good if they are lived day by day. Well, goodbye now."

"Wait a minute, please. Don't leave yet. Anyway, I want to know what the principles are."

"They are ten principles of marriage that may seem obvious when you hear them, but you would think that they were secret because most people don't know them."

"Oh, please tell me. Tell me what they are..." Sarah pleaded eagerly.

"Like I said, I don't want to waste your time or mine unless you are willing to commit to do every assignment that I give you."

Sarah paused, hung her head and closed her eyes for what seemed like an endless amount of time. When she raised her head, her eyes met mine with a penetrating gaze. "Like you said, it's all about priorities in life. I guess it's about time I made my marriage a priority rather than putting it last on my list and never getting to it. Okay," she sighed. "I give you my word of honor that I'll do the assignments. Will you start with me until I can talk to my husband about this? I'm just promising for myself."

"That's good enough to get started," I assured her. She smiled, relieved.

I let Elisabeth out of the stroller again, and sat down on the couch. I said a silent prayer that I would be able to help Sarah and that she would be humble enough to learn.

"So... What's secret number one for achieving a successful celestial marriage?"

"Secret number one is actually five secrets all in one package. I call it the *Five Pillars of a Celestial Marriage*."

"I've never heard of 'em. What are they?"

"They're daily and weekly habits in a marriage that form the foundation of a loving relationship between a husband and wife. The first pillar is nightly couple's prayer.

"How's that going to help us? We have family prayer with the kids already every night. Isn't that enough?"

"It's admirable that you have regular family prayer. Prayer will create a special spirit in the home for your children and teach them how important their relationship is with Father in Heaven. But what about you and your husband, and your relationship with the Lord as a couple?"

"I don't understand."

"You and your husband need your own special time with the Lord away from the children, where you can pour out your hearts to Him about things that are inappropriate for them to hear."

"Oh, we tried that once but there wasn't really anything to say after our family prayer with the kids."

"Do you have a personal prayer to the Lord each night?"

"Of course. In fact the Lord is probably tired of hearing me complain about my husband."

"Sounds as if you have developed a special relationship with the

Lord alone. You trust Him. You pour out your heart to Him."

"Yeah, exactly."

"What's missing from your marriage is that same feeling you have when you say your prayers to the Lord by yourself. You need to have that same openness and oneness with the Lord in a nightly, couple's prayer with your husband. Remember when you were married in the temple?"

"Sure. It was a dream come true."

"What were your hopes and dreams about your marriage?"

"That we'd always be united."

"That's what all couples want. They start out hoping that their marriage will be filled with love and unity. And this can happen. In fact, the goal of a temple marriage is to strive for oneness in spirit. However, this can only occur if you are holding nightly couple's prayer. In the sanctity of your own bedroom, you should kneel down together at the side of your bed and envision yourself literally entering the presence of the Lord."

"Wow. It sounds like preparing to go to the temple."

"Exactly. Your couple's prayer should be a sacred time for you and your husband. It's a time to develop spiritual oneness with each other and the Lord."

"I wish somebody had told me to do this before."

"It's not too late to start."

"Do you and your husband have a couple's prayer every night?"

"We couldn't live without it. You see, we are striving to achieve a true celestial marriage on earth. In the temple, we are promised that we can achieve this goal, but we have to work at it. And the first step is developing a relationship with the Lord together."

"But what do you talk about? It seems like so many of our prayers are automatic and almost memorized clichés."

"You're not alone. Lots of people get into speaking ruts while they pray, or they're in a hurry and just want to get it over with so they can either go to sleep or watch a late night TV show. When my husband and I say our couple's prayer, it is a reminder of where we came from and why we are here on earth. It helps us focus on the important issues of life rather than the mundane and petty. We literally feel as if we are reporting in to Heavenly Father about our life together. Sometimes we feel almost as if He were really in the room with us. We discuss with the Lord our goals and ask for His help. We are always very specific. We never hesitate to talk about what we are going to do to improve our relationship with each other. Sometimes as we have ended the prayer, a thought will run through our minds from the Spirit inspiring us with ideas of what we need to do. It is incredible when it happens to us simultaneously. After exchanging our inspirations, we hug and kiss and feel so close to each other. It's at times like that when we know we are on the pathway to achieving a true celestial marriage."

Elisabeth walked up and handed me a block. "Thank you, honey," I said. "Can you give that to Lily?"

"But what if your husband is saying the prayer and he doesn't say the things you want him to? I mean... you know... maybe you want to talk to the Lord about helping you to not criticize each other, and he doesn't say anything about it when he knows we have that problem?"

"Well, we're creative. If that should happen to us, I will squeeze my husband's hand before he can close the prayer. Then I start talking to the Lord, adding other concerns and end the prayer myself. Whether it's me adding to my husband's prayer or my husband adding to my prayer, it's a great feeling. It always makes me feel as if we are in a joint conversation with the Lord."

"Why do you hold each other's hands when you pray together?" Sarah asked.

"It symbolizes togetherness and our goal to become one in spirit."

"That makes sense."

"This habit is a fundamental of a celestial marriage and will change your life together."

"You think so?"

"I know so. It will take time. Its effect is long term and cumulative. You must start at the beginning to develop a spiritual bond together and with the Lord."

"I'm beginning to see the benefits."

"So far, I've emphasized the spiritual benefits. Practically speaking, I find it is impossible to go to bed mad at my husband. You see, I know I must report in to the Lord each night. Facing this nightly interview with Him makes petty differences, stresses of the day, arguments, and differences of opinion melt away. Our couple's prayer always gets us drawn back to what is really important in our relationship, and that is achieving oneness with each other and the Lord."

"I can't wait to get started tonight. I'm already feeling happier."

"Amazing what a little hope can do to brighten our day."

"You said there were 'Five Pillars of a Celestial Marriage.' You've only told me one. What are the other four?"

"Pillar number two of a celestial marriage is *Daily Talk Time*."

"What is *Daily Talk Time*?"

"Do you remember when you were courting and you couldn't wait to call your fiancèe when you got home from school or work? Words would flow freely and easily as each of you listened unconditionally to each other. During these conversations you would share: the events of the day, frustrating moments, triumphs, philosophical thoughts and feelings, and ideas for solving problems. Talk time wasn't a formal event. It just happened because you considered each other the top priority."

"That's one reason I fell in love with my husband. He made me feel that I was the most important part of his life."

"Unfortunately, in our high paced society, and as we face more and more demands on our time, it's easy to forego conversations with our mate. Some couples turn on the TV, radio, or stereo in an effort to unwind. You have children, so you understand how easy it is to live with your husband, and not talk to him for days on end other than: 'See you after my meetings,' 'Be sure and take the dog to the vet today,' or 'Remember Susie's violin concert at 8:00pm. Meet you there.'"

"Sounds like you've been watching a secret video tape of our family."

"I have frequently been at dinner parties during which a spouse will tell about an interesting experience that occurred to him or her, and the other spouse will say, 'You never told me that! When did it happen?' I always think to myself, 'Hmm I guess they don't have daily talk time.' Of course, there are exceptions. We might forget during talk time to tell our mate about an experience because our minds are filled with so many things to talk about. However, if this is a frequent occurrence, my guess would be that the couple isn't really having a 'Daily Talk Time.'"

"My sister, Betsy, and her husband, Bob, started a tradition of taking nightly walks together during which they had their daily talk time. When they came home to visit us on holidays, they would still take their nightly walks alone. I admired their unity. Little did my older sister and her husband know the wonderful example they were setting for me. Although my sister never referred to their walks as a 'Talk Time,' I knew what they were doing. They needed their time to be alone together. In my parents' generation they called this tradition 'Pillow Talk.' It was the time they could talk openly without little children's ears listening. I still remember my mother telling me how important that time was that she had with my father.

"You will remember many sweet moments during your courtship when you shared frustrating moments of the day with your fiancèe. And, the love of your life would never let you down. He would always sympathize with you and say, 'I know what you mean. I feel the same way. Wow! We're so alike. Oh, I love you so much! Thanks for always being there for me. You are the only person who really understands me!' *This is what talk time is all about!* It is finding the time each day to give your spouse a chance to talk about his or her frustrations or disappointments, and then sympathizing and giving them the verbal support and love that they so desperately need."

"That's exactly what I long for in our marriage. Instead, it seems that anything I say turns into a fight," Sarah lamented.

"I find it is utterly amazing that spouses who were so understanding before marriage, taking as much time as was needed to listen to their fiancèe's frustrations, after a few years into the marriage, are too busy to listen to a spouse's concerns. Somehow, the spouse takes second place to TV, projects around the house, golf with buddies, girl's or boy's night out, meetings, and children's needs, when they used to be the number one priority."

"That's our trouble. We are so busy we don't have time to talk. And when we do, we are in a hurry to spit it all out. Then the fight happens."

"When you were dating, did you ever call your true love during the day, in between classes or on a break from work, just to find out what was happening?"

Sarah nodded in agreement.

"You were so in love, you couldn't bear to wait until the end of the day to talk, to listen to his voice, to share his frustrations or revel in his success. Or, perhaps you called him to tell that you were bursting with happiness from your new promotion, or getting an 'A' on your final exam. At the end of day you might have heard the sentence: 'I am so happy for you. Tell me the whole event detail by detail all over again.' And then, your fiancèe would smile at you and give you loving looks as you repeated the entire story all over again. *This is talk time!* Unfortunately, all too frequently, some couples who have been married for a few years no longer take the time to listen to each other, or even revel in the other one's success."

"I'm really guilty of that. I haven't been excited about anything my husband has done lately when I should have been. I've been concentrating on the negative I guess. Now I can't wait until he comes home so that I can plan a talk time with him. I've got some catching up to do."

"My favorite part of dating with my husband was sharing our philosophical thoughts and then discussing these views with him. This is a way most couples start out. They share their thoughts on spirituality, raising children, politics, etc. All too frequently, they think they know their mate and don't need to discuss these things after they are married. In their minds people are static and remain the same. How grateful I am that my husband needed talk time as much as I did. In fact, over the years we have spent many stimulating hours learning and discussing new philosophies. We both say unanimously that we developed our political philosophy together by reading books, taking seminars together, and having hours of wonderful talk time discussing, debating, and drawing conclusions. This kind of talk time has brought us closer together than we ever were in our courtship. Sometimes we would disagree with each other and enjoy a lively but friendly debate. If we ended up agreeing after the discussion, we'd usually hug and express the joy we felt in our relationship. When we didn't agree at the end of our discussion we would laugh, hug each other, and say something that would make the other person laugh. *This is talk time!*

"When the deaths of Princess Diana and Mother Teresa occurred, I needed to talk. I needed to sift through the world's views versus mine. I felt that the world worshipped youth and beauty. Diana was an impressive person, but I was tired of hearing the words 'Saint Diana' when her charity efforts were part of her job as royalty. She was paid every year by the taxpayers to live in eight different palaces and appear at charities. Then Mother Teresa died. Her works were indisputably noble. But again, it was her job. She never married, had children, or held a full time job in addition to raising a family. Being a nun was her profession. I wanted to discuss the meaning of being a saint. I thought of church members who work full-time, have families, attend PTA, volunteer in the community, and yet find time to counsel the troubled, visit the sick, take in meals, serve as volunteers at church, and help their neighbors. Church members volunteer regularly without any publicity, financial compensation, or other reward. To me the true saints in life are Latter Day-Saints, appropriately named. My husband readily agreed and said, 'I love you honey. You always have such incredible insights.' *This is talk time: Listening and being in awe of your mate!*"

"I can't believe how something so simple can be so profound."

"Finally, talk time is discussing solutions to problems. It is having brain storming sessions and never putting down each other's ideas. It is being humble and open to your spouse's thoughts and feelings in solving a problem together. It is making decisions and then praying about them together."

"Our time together talking is mostly shouting," Sarah added.

"Oh," I said inhaling. I remembered a list I give my class members about talk time, and what it is not. I reviewed the ideas with Sarah.

TALK TIME IS SHARING YOUR SOULS, MINDS, AND SPIRITS, HEART TO HEART.

Some couples insist that they have daily talk time and truly they do. So why aren't they happy? Here is a list of what talk time is *not!*

1. Saying, "yeah, yeah, I've heard you say that a thousand times," and walking off in a huff.
2. Listening to your mate tell about an accomplishment and saying, "A little over done don't you think," and walking off preoccupied with your own self.
3. Saying, "Are you done? Good, because I've got things to do."
4. Saying, "I don't know where you come up with such hare-brained ideas."
5. Saying, "If you'd just listen to me, we'd be fine. You just don't get it, do you? Okay, I'm just going to have to do it by myself."

"Sarah, these are only a few of the don'ts. There are many things that we can say to turn off our mates and discourage them from talking to us about what is important to their feelings, dreams, and goals. But, even if we have some negatives creep into our talk time, it's still more important to keep on talking, and not allow those negative moments to stop us."

WHAT HAPPENS WITHOUT TALK TIME?

"Your mate will find someone else to talk to. Simple. Some will find a friend of their own sex. You've all heard about friends who tell all of the faults of their spouse to a girlfriend or colleague and complain endlessly. This habit further drives a wedge into the husband and wife relationship. Then...

WORSE THINGS CAN HAPPEN:

"Your mate will find someone else of the opposite sex to confide in: a co-worker, someone on the internet, an old girlfriend/boyfriend, someone from church, or a friend at an athletic club. They will talk on the telephone or the internet daily to this special someone who soon becomes a girlfriend/boyfriend. After months of daily talk time with another, temptations increase, adultery often follows, then divorce, and the cycle starts again.

"Last summer I called up Phil and Tami to invite them to a dinner party. Tami sounded so happy. In fact, she was unusually happy. I said, 'Tami what's happening? You are happier than I've heard you sound in ten years.' Gushing with enthusiasm, she revealed, 'I reunited with my high school sweetheart last summer at our twentieth reunion. Since then, we've been communicating via e-mail. In fact, every day!' Tami worked as a graphic artist out of her home. She earned a sizable income planning the layout, paste-up, and illustrations of several regional magazines. Her husband traveled an average of two weeks out of every month in a high-powered executive job. Phil and Tami had their differences like any normal couple. And now Tami, who needed talk time with a friend, a confidant, and especially someone of the opposite sex, had started a mental affair. It was just a matter of time before the mental affair would turn into a sexual one.

"Lest you think that this only happens to non-LDS, think again. A married woman named Karen, called for advice. She said that she was falling in love with a friend of the family, a married man named Stuart. Karen and her husband, Steve, had been married in the Temple and had four children. Over the last 20 years of marriage, romance had ceased and talk time was non-existent. Steve wouldn't listen to Karen's concerns and complaints, or even her dreams and goals. Stuart, on the other hand, was home during the day, and would often call Karen on the phone and listen to her. He had free time because he was currently unemployed, and living off a grant which he had secured for the planning phase of an expedition to climb the seven highest mountains in the world. He hoped to raise the rest of the funding from private corporations. Stuart's wife did not understand his dreams. She had agonized over every previous mountain he had climbed from Denali to Mt. Rainier. She resented his time away from home and the money he spent on climbing instead of on his family. Stuart's wife frequently accused him of being selfish. As you can imagine, they too stopped talking to each other.

"Soon, Karen began to verbally support Stuart on the phone by sharing in his dream. She suggested he write a book about his adventures. Stuart did not include his wife in most of his decisions. He told Karen that his wife didn't care. He misread his wife's negative reactions as apathy. They were actually just a result of a lack of communication and talk time. Karen, on the other hand, was his cheerleader. Stuart was thrilled to receive this support and inspiration, and Karen was happy to give it. Karen's husband seemed to squelch all her desires. Now she had someone to share her dreams. Karen and Stuart were two lonely souls in need of talk time. Each wanted a friend who would give unconditional love. That friend should have been a spouse. At first, Karen's telephone conversations with Stuart were perfectly innocent, support for a man with an exciting goal. But as the months passed by, the friendship had turned into love that neither of them was receiving at home.

"When Karen came to me for advice, I remember telling her to go on a date with her husband and talk this out before it was too late. With a prayer in her heart and the help of the Lord she was to express her love to her husband, inform him of the budding romance with Stuart, and ask her husband to love and support her in the way in which she needed it. The object was to assure Steve that she loved him and that she needed and wanted daily talk time, and a close relationship with him, not Stuart.

Karen promised to telephone me two weeks later with a full report on this assignment. Weeks passed by without a call from Karen. The weeks turned into months. When I finally connected with Karen, it was too late. She had begun a physical affair with Stuart. I begged her to cut it off, tell her husband, and seek counseling to bring her marriage back to where it had started. She finally confronted Steve, but now there was too much that had happened, and it appeared that reconciliation was impossible.

"Unfortunately Steve didn't understand. He blamed Stuart. He blamed Karen. He couldn't see that he had a part in driving his wife into the arms of another by refusing to give her the kind of love that she needed. If they had only lived the 'Five Pillars of a Celestial Marriage,' they could have avoided the tangled web of adultery and the ultimate decline of their marriage."

Sarah had been listening intently through my long lecture, when she interjected: "OK, I see how important it is, but how do you do it? What do you do when your husband closes you off? What if it's something you've heard a thousand times before?"

"Let me give you some examples. One day Conrad and I took a walk down by the stream in our backyard. At this time of our lives we were both booked solid with work, church, and filming documentaries. We sat down by the outdoor fireplace hoping to just talk for a few minutes. Conrad started first. As he talked, it sounded like a familiar theme I had heard from him before. He was in a philosophical mood. I was anxious to talk about my problem of the day. I found myself unable to listen and I was short with him. Suddenly I caught myself and apologized. I told him that I was impatient because all I could do was think about my problem that needed solving. He gallantly told me to please go ahead and tell him my situation. I did. He was sympathetic and loving. He satisfied my needs and I was happy. Then he had his turn. I was able to listen with true empathy. We embraced, feeling like we were loved, and that we were the luckiest people in the world to have a best friend who just happened to also be our spouse.

"On another occasion I was preparing my lesson for my Celestial Marriage class on Talk Time. I was so excited and wanted to share this principle with Conrad. It was Saturday morning and he had things to do. I said, 'Conrad listen to this!' and I read a few phrases from my writing. He walked off hastily and uttered, 'Yeah, I've already heard that.' I actually laughed as he walked away. I called him back and thanked him for giving me material for my class. I told him that he had just done what you're not supposed to do as a married couple. He laughed, realizing what he had said. Then he replied, 'Sorry honey. I really did hear what you said. And you know what? You are truly inspired!' Then he kissed me and said, 'I'd like to hear more when I can focus. How about tonight during our talk time.' I was on cloud nine. Amazing what a little positive talk will do.

Sarah was crying again.

"I'm sorry. Did I say something to hurt you?"

"Oh, no. You're inspiring me. Please continue."

"Just remember that the keys to talk time are: *Humility and unconditional, non-judgemental listening skills.* Let's go on to pillar number three."

"Wait a minute, I'm going to start taking notes."

Sarah ran to the kitchen and returned soberly with a notebook and pen. "Okay I'm ready."

"Pillar number three is: *Have a weekly date with your spouse.* Now this weekly date does not mean going to a church potluck dinner where one talks to everybody but his or her spouse. A couple's date means just the two of you. This ensures constant romance, togetherness, a deepening of the relationship, sharing of each other's interests, and growing together away from the children. A weekly date is a strong recommendation from the Church. One time in my marriage class I asked people to raise their hands if they thought that 'Family Home Evening' was a modern day commandment from the Lord. All hands were raised in the affirmative. The class knew that Prophet David O. McKay had foreseen the television set replacing good old-fashioned family games and togetherness. Many families I know today have three TV sets in the house. On weekends, the family rents three movies: one for the teens, one for the parents, and one for the little ones. Then they all separate into different rooms. Even the nightly family meal has almost become obsolete, with each family member on a different schedule.

Families, it seems, have practically become a member of the 'endangered species list.' Prophet McKay foresaw the family becoming more and more separated from each other. It was time for the Lord to reveal a new commandment to get people to spend time with their families on a designated day. This program had actually been around since the early 1900's, but by the Fifties, it became necessary for it to be a modern day commandment. The Lord knew of the coming disintegration of the family. In bygone eras, it wasn't necessary to have a commandment telling people that they needed to spend time together. People didn't have TVs, CD players, VCRs and personal computers to compete for time with the family. Their evenings were spent reading together, playing games and doing other in-home activities. Families were together most evenings by default. Travel was difficult and a plethora of outside enticements did not exist for the common man. Family Home Evening would ensure togetherness and unity for at least one night a week while creating an atmosphere of security, love, and quality communications.

"So too, in our day, the Lord foresaw the eroding of the relationship between husband and wife. In 1976, Elder L. Tom Perry spent time training the new stake presidency of the Seattle North Stake: President Brent Nash, First Counselor Russ Nickel, and Second Counselor Jim Nelson. Relating to the training session, Brother Nickel stressed, 'In October 1976, Elder Perry included a calendar guide to help us accomplish everything. The first two things on the calendar were: Family Home Evening on Monday night, and Date with Wife, on Friday night.' The Seattle North Stake followed General Authority, Elder L. Tom Perry's directive to set aside Friday as the designated dating night to be held sacred for married couples, and Monday night for Family Home Evening.

"My husband and I worked on a PBS National Documentary called *Children of Divorce*. During the interviews, I learned how important a weekly date is in a marriage. All too many couples grow apart and eliminate romance altogether. Their marriages sink to the level of a husband being merely a wage earner and the wife a meal provider. Then when a handsome hunk or blushing beauty flirts with them on a PTA committee or at work, the excitement of a budding romance can be fatal.

"One wife complained to me that her husband would come home from work, boot up his computer and talk on chat lines until long after she had gone to bed. This went on for several years. They were practically strangers to each other. She felt neglected, put upon and found herself in the trap of nagging him for attention. How sad it was! If only he had followed the recommendation to take her out on a weekly date. There are few members of the church who wouldn't unequivocally agree that to hold Family Home Evening is a necessity to keep families together. *But...* do people in the church really realize that to go on a weekly date with their spouse is just as important as Family Home Evening? Without a strong married couple's relationship, children lack good examples, and have the potential of growing up in a dysfunctional home. As a result, children may later lack the skills themselves to develop celestial marriages."

Sarah's almond shaped brown eyes glittered with excitement. "This is just what we need. I need to feel special and like I'm being courted again. So, the first pillar of celestial marriage is to have a couple's prayer every night. I'm writing these down. Then number two is to have daily talk time and number three is to have a weekly date.

"Wow!" Sarah exclaimed. "Elder Perry, who represented the Prophet when he was training those leaders, certainly made it crystal clear. A date is equally as important as Family Home Evening. And everyone knows that Family Home Evening is like a modern day commandment. Wait 'til I tell Jake that we have to have a weekly date! He'll be thrilled. He's always trying to get me to get babysitters so that we can get out alone, just the two of us."

"The fourth pillar of a celestial marriage on earth is to *have a weekly planning session with your spouse*. My husband and I have found Sunday evening to be the best time to go over our commitments for the week. This habit eliminates many an argument when one mate says to the other, 'How could you forget Jenny's basketball game?' 'You never told me it was tonight.' 'Oh, you are too much. I told you when you were in the shower three weeks ago that tonight was the night.' This kind of interaction can easily be avoided if the husband and wife have a weekly planning session and write the week's activities and events on their respective calendars. It's thoughtless of a spouse to assume that his or her spouse will remember an event that hasn't been written down. Anyone who has been on a mission knows the value of weekly planning with a companion. It's a habit to be carried into one's marriage and circumvents scheduling disappointments and nightmare conflicts."

"That's one pillar of marriage that we actually do! My husband learned that habit on his mission and we have always been good at scheduling with each other."

"Terrific! You're one step ahead of thousands of other couples."

"I can't wait to hear what the last pillar of a celestial marriage is."

"The fifth pillar of a celestial marriage is to *study the scriptures together*. Realistically, I ask my couples in my Sunday School class to read the scriptures together only four nights a week for five to ten minutes, and then discuss their ideas and thoughts. In one of my classes the couples were all newlyweds. They thought that only four nights a week for ten minutes at a time was too easy. Since then, many of them have given birth to two or more children. Their tune has changed. They insist, now, that I knew what I was talking about. They are so busy in their complex lives, four nights a week is a lot. But... they always say, just those five minutes draw them closer together spiritually. Sometimes, it even answers problems they have been praying about together.

"It is amazing what you can accomplish in a short amount of time. One year Conrad and I decided to study the Doctrine and Covenants together. We were lucky if we had five minutes at a time. And yet, we had some great discussions. During that year we studied many scriptures from the Doctrine and Covenants. To help us remember them, we gave each section a catchy title – "Prayer," or "The Worth of Souls," or "Degrees of Glory." It was fun and gave us a sense of accomplishment together. Some couples ask me why family scripture reading wouldn't be enough. It is, if the couple also has private time together to discuss, on a mature level, the scriptures they read with their children. Some couples are so pressed for time that they read assigned scriptures separately during the day, and then discuss it together for five or ten minutes along with their talk time. The purpose of reading scriptures as a couple is to help them grow together spiritually."

"Jerry and Rachael were referred to me by their Bishop for spiritual counseling. They were an outstanding couple who had been in a serious auto accident. Unfortunately, it had left the husband paralyzed from the waist down. For six months the husband had wallowed in self-pity. He wouldn't get dressed in the morning. He wouldn't shave. He just booted up his computer and played mindless games all day long. He was so depressed that Rachael finally went to the Bishop, who recommended they come to me for help. Jerry willingly agreed. After meeting them, I could tell that the last thing Jerry wanted was a lecture. He had been raised in the church, had been on a mission, and had served as the Elders Quorum President. This was an outstanding man whose life had been turned upside down. What do you think he needed?

"From what you've been telling me, I guess the 'Five Pillars of a Celestial Marriage?'"

"Yes. But which one do you think I asked them to live first?"

"Talk time?"

"Jerry really needed talk time to be sure, but he had refused to open up to his wife. She tried to get him to talk about his feelings but he resented it. Try again?"

"Couple's daily prayer?"

"That is a good answer. Unfortunately, at this time in Jerry's life, he didn't want to pray to the Lord. Any prayer with his wife seemed like a form of manipulation to him. I only asked them to do one thing: read the scriptures every day that week including a subsequent couple's discussion. Jerry agreed. The next week when they came to see me, Jerry had a big smile on his face. He was filled with light and hope. Finally he had begun filling his mind with positive writings instead of mindless activities that augmented his unhappiness. Their discussions became the highlight of Jerry's day. The next week I was able to add talk time to scriptural reading. They understood that this talk time was in addition to discussing the scriptures. Rachael was sensitive to Jerry and refrained from prodding him to share his feelings of self-worth since the accident. Instead she talked about what mattered to her. And as we all know, after we listen to others talk about themselves for a long time, we feel the need to talk about ourselves in order to get a little attention. The plan worked. Jerry began to open up to Rachael. They grieved together about his loss of physical abilities from the accident. They found new goals together. They developed plans for living with Jerry's disability. Of course, with the addition of couple's prayer, Jerry became close to his wife and the Lord again. Finally the date night brought romance back into Jerry's life when he thought that he was useless as a romantic partner. Week by week, and month by month, Jerry and Rachael were on the way once again to a celestial marriage on earth.

Sarah looked pensive. "What are you thinking, Sarah?" I quizzed.

"You made me realize how important it is to read the scriptures to fill our minds with uplifting messages. Just like Jerry needed powerful stories and inspiration to pull him out of his troubles, I think about how important it is to our marriage. You know, on dates even."

"That's very perceptive of you, Sarah. Each time I go out to dinner with my husband I always spot at least one or two couples who don't seem to have anything to say to each other. They stare into space, watch other couples, and eat in silence. These are couples who don't read scriptures or, in the least, uplifting literature or self-help books that they can share and discuss with their mate on a date. Even after many years of marriage we like to share what we've been studying or reading. It is so stimulating to share new information, ask our loved one's opinion, and enjoy the interchange of ideas."

"That makes so much sense. So many times I've nagged my husband. Rather than preparing myself with some interesting reading to talk about, I've said, 'why don't you talk to me? Say something.' Of course that always makes him mad and then he doesn't want to talk with me at all." Sarah admitted sheepishly.

"I'm so happy that you have been able to see several reasons why it is important to read the scriptures and discuss them together as a couple.

"At different times in our marriages, one of the 'Five Pillars of a Celestial Marriage' will be more important to the marriage than another. In any case, setting up a pattern of living them day by day and week by week ensures that we have a system in place and ready to go when the vicissitudes of life hit us the hardest.

"In review, the 'Five Pillars of a Celestial Marriage' are:"

THE FIVE PILLARS OF A CELESTIAL MARRIAGE

1.   Have a nightly couple's prayer, holding hands.

2.   Have a daily talk time.

3.   Have a weekly date.

4.   Hold a weekly planning session every Sunday evening.

5.   Read the scriptures together and discuss the passages a minimum of 5-10 minutes, four times a week.

"Okay, " Sarah asked, "if I practice the 'Five Pillars of a Celestial Marriage' with my husband, how long will it take before all of our problems are solved?"

"Wait a minute," I demurred. "If you practice them faithfully, you will have the foundation for solving all of your problems. Remember, I told you there were ten secrets? This is only one of them. When you're doing the 'Five Pillars' faithfully, you will need to start practicing the other nine secrets for achieving a successful celestial marriage."

"Okay, now you've got me hooked." She sat back down at the table and took up her pen again. "What are the other nine?"

I had to laugh. "No, I think that's plenty for today. I need to know you can do the first step before I help you any farther down the road. Give me a call when you've managed to have couples' prayer and talk time every night for a week, plus scripture study four nights, a date and a planning session, all in the same week. Then I'll come over and give you the second secret."

I stood up and stretched my legs, then looked around for Elisabeth. She and Lily had fallen asleep on the floor next to the pile of blocks! At least she wouldn't be cranky that night because she hadn't had a nap. I picked her up and carefully strapped her into the stroller.

Sarah opened the door for us. "Thank you," she said.

"You're welcome," I replied, "but thank me when your marriage is back in order."

"Don't worry," she said, her face an odd mixture of delight and determination. "You'll be hearing back from me soon."

Fortunately, the dark clouds had cleared and I arrived at home a few minutes later, chilled but dry. As I started getting the ingredients together for dinner, I planned the next lesson for Sarah and her husband. I had a feeling I would be giving it soon.

ASSIGNMENT NUMBER ONE:

Live the *Five Pillars of a Successful Celestial Marriage* daily and weekly. To start, practice by living them all faithfully for at least one full week. Commit to do so for the rest of your lives.

CHAPTER 2

KNOW YOUR MISSION

E lisabeth's little legs ran almost faster than I could keep up. She squealed with glee, knowing she was going to play with Lily. Although my visit was service oriented, the benefit of a new playmate for Elisabeth was a blessing for me.

"Just talk," Sarah blurted out. "I'm your devoted pupil."

As if I was giving a talk at Stake Conference, I launched into the second secret of achieving a successful celestial marriage. Time is a factor when two-year-olds are playing. Who knew how long their attention would be occupied in harmonious play?

I began my oration. "It is a beautiful sight to observe a young couple in love. They hang on each other's every word. Their facial expressions are filled with endless smiles and eyes twinkling with unconditional love. They touch each other tentatively and then tenderly, careful not to offend. These couples have one thought: the happiness of their sweetheart. They wouldn't dream of doing anything to knowingly hurt the love of their life. One false move would risk losing the union they so desire. Declaring undying loyalty and devotion to each other is a given, and there is nothing that they wouldn't do to fulfill each other's dreams. Too often, however, relationships that start out on this highest plane of love end up in the garbage dump without even the minimum option of recycling.

"The second secret to a successful celestial marriage on earth is to discover your spouse's gifts and talents and potential missions on earth, and then to do everything in your power to help him or her accomplish them."

"How can I possibly know that? I can't see into the future," Sarah blurted out.

"Ah, but the Lord can. Your Patriarchal Blessing and your husband's Patriarchal Blessing are the blueprints to your potential missions on earth."

"What do you mean?"

"Some people think that their Patriarchal Blessing belongs only to them and is only for them. But when we learn that a celestial marriage is a partnership, it becomes clear that the blessings that are promised to your spouse are also promised to you."

"I never thought of it that way. But when I hear you say it, it makes sense. When my husband gets a raise, I get a raise, more money in our household account."

"That's right."

"But, when I was called to be a primary teacher, I always wanted my husband to draw visual aids for the class. I could never get him away from the TV to do them for me. He's a great artist, but he thought it was a waste of time."

"That's where Patriarchal Blessings come in. What does yours say about your teaching?"

"It says that I will be a teacher to the little children in the wards of Zion."

"If only your husband had known that this calling was part of your mission in life, he would have caught the vision and supported you."

"You think so?"

"Yes. I do."

"My husband and I have different gifts. He is blessed with the gift of discernment. He knows if people are sincere, if they are lying, or if they are what they claim to be. Not me! I tend to look at life through rose colored glasses. Knowing that my husband had this gift when we first were married has been a great asset to me. I rely on his assessments and know that he is there to help me whenever I need him. In like manner, I have the gift of pure faith. Early on in our marriage, my husband would rely on my faith when we needed answers to prayers. By knowing each other's gifts and relying on them, we have been able to augment our own abilities. Now my husband has developed his own great faith and I am developing discernment. By fostering and admiring our spouse's gifts and relying on them in times of need, we move towards a true partnership. As we perfect ourselves, we can develop these same gifts by mentoring each other."

"I don't mean to change the subject, but I still don't really understand the basic difference between a celestial marriage and an earthly one."

"Obviously, the first difference is that a celestial marriage starts in the temple and is for time and all eternity. A secular marriage is only until 'death do you part.' An earthly marriage is one that is of the world between two people. A celestial marriage literally has God as a third partner.

"Most importantly, the difference between an earthly marriage and a celestial eternal one is that a celestial marriage involves a special vision of each other. It means that you see each other through God's eyes. You see each other's greatness and seek to help your partner accomplish his or her mission on earth. You are God's partner in bringing to pass your spouse's mission on earth. If you are supportive, you can help him achieve his potential. If not, you can actually thwart the purposes of God."

"Then being selfish or squelching your spouse's potential is really serious."

"Yes. Unfortunately, many husbands and wives are only focused on themselves and their own desires, to the neglect and even prevention of their spouse's purpose on earth. It is a hideous thought, but so common in the world. A worldly marriage is selfish, 'me' focused, and unbending. A celestial marriage is selfless, sacrificing, and focused on your one and only love. A celestial marriage is non-judgmental, slow to anger, and never criticizes. A worldly marriage can be filled with criticism and negative behavior that slowly tears away at a partner's self-esteem and ability to achieve. Spouses in that kind of a worldly marriage use their partner for their own self gratification, never giving thought to the husband's or wife's development.

"A celestial marriage always seeks to see one's partner through God's all-knowing eyes. If a husband knew that his wife was going to discover the cure for cancer, he wouldn't dream of standing in her way. In fact he would go out of his way to support her, thereby becoming a partner, helping to accomplish her mission to humanity. His support would manifest itself in many ways. For example, he might babysit the children some evenings so that she could spend a few more hours doing research at the office."

"You give me chills. But what about the men who think that they are the only ones who could possibly have a career or mission that matters?"

"Prophet Gordon B. Hinckley, September 28, 1985 at the General Woman's Meeting reminded us: 'It was Florence Nightengale, the frail English girl, who out of a great sense of concern, went to the Crimea and nursed the wounded, and out of whose efforts has grown the great international Red Cross.'[1] Florence Nightengale's contribution to the world is indisputable. The mission she served to humanity was indeed serving the Lord.

[1] Prophet Gordon B. Hinckley, "Ten Gifts From The Lord" (*Ensign*, November 1985) pgs. 86-89

"I often think of Marie Osmond who had a mission to the world as a singer and representative of the Church. While I was on my mission in France, one of the ways we could get people to invite us into their home was to mention that Marie Osmond was a Mormon.

"Suddenly they would become interested. They wanted to know what Marie Osmond's religion was all about. So you see, Marie Osmond not only served a mission in the world with her singing talent, but she also served a spiritual mission. Doors opened up to missionaries all over the world because of Marie Osmond and her brothers. However, she could not have fulfilled her mission in life if she didn't have the support of her family, who recognized that women have missions that need to be discovered and fulfilled on earth."

"I guess that says it all."

"Prophet Gordon B. Hinckley, in the same 1985 address at the General Women's Meeting said, 'Your potential is limitless. You are daughters of God, endowed by inheritance with marvelous gifts and immeasurable potential.' Of course, that doesn't mean that women should pursue a career selfishly any more than a man should. We must always do things for the right reasons."

"What are those?"

"If we can serve the Lord."

"You mean if you are like Marie Osmond and have the gift to sing and an opportunity to be a great example to the world, you should do it? You know... and ignore the cultural pressures of being in the home full time?"

"Yes, of course, if you have prayed about it, and received a personal revelation that it is right for you and your husband. Prayer and personal revelation are the bottom line to discovering your missions in life. At the same time, one must clearly know that most missions are not like Marie Osmond's. Most will receive no recognition in this life. They include the quiet service given to others. They are the selfless acts of motherhood, nurturing and instilling values in the heroes and heroines of tomorrow.

"My second cousin, Carl Nelson, who lived in a suburb of New York City for many years, developed the use of microfilm in the work place. His contribution to the world is widely recognized. But he never could have achieved such success without the team effort support of his wife. He had four small children at home. Their exuberance and desire to play with Daddy interfered with his goal to write the definitive book on microfilm. His wife suggested that he take an apartment in Manhattan, only coming home on the weekends. This way he could spend every possible waking hour after work writing a book that would lead the rest of the world in the science of microfilm. He followed her suggestion and McGraw Hill published his voluminous work a year and a half later. His mission was accomplished by a team effort with his wife."

"Gosh, I wouldn't let my husband live away from us for a year and a half, and only come home on weekends, to write a book," Sarah whined closed-mindedly.

"The point is that we all have missions on earth to fulfill, but we cannot accomplish them without the loving support of our spouse."

Sarah looked at me sheepishly.

I continued. "We know for a fact that God knew all of us in the pre-mortal world. We are His literal sons and daughters. Abraham had a vision in which he saw the spirit world. In the *Pearl of Great Price*, the Book of Abraham 3: 22-23, it says: 'Now the Lord had shown unto me, Abraham, the intelligences that were organized before the world was; and among all these there were many of the noble and great ones. And God saw these souls that were good and He stood in the midst of them, and He said: These I will make my rulers; for He stood among those that were spirits and He saw that they were good; and He said unto me: Abraham, thou art one of them; thou wast chosen before thou wast born.'"

"You mean many of us were foreordained to specific missions on earth?" Sarah asked.

"Here it is in black and white," I noted. "Jeremiah was told directly from the Lord that he was foreordained to be a prophet on earth! In the Old Testament, Jeremiah 1: 5, it says: "Before I formed thee in the belly I knew thee; and before thou camest forth out of the womb I sanctified thee, and I ordained thee a prophet unto the nations."

"My father was told in his Patriarchal Blessing that he would be called to be a Judge in Israel where he would establish peace, harmony, and unity in a ward filled with contention and strife. As a result of his leadership many miracles would occur among the people. It came true in 1950 when he was called to be the Bishop of a Puget Sound Ward. Even the calling in and of itself was miraculous. There had been such dissension in this ward, that when the previous Bishop was sustained and the Stake President said, 'All opposed please raise their hands,' half of the members voted against him. My parents, who were newcomers to The Puget Sound area, witnessed this unusual event first hand. Later, the Stake Presidency returned to the area knowing that they needed Heavenly Father's direct inspiration to know who should be the next

Bishop, a man who could bring peace, harmony, and unity to this ailing body of people. With prayers in their hearts, each member of the Seattle Stake Presidency was inspired to meet my father, ask him his name, shake his hand, and feel by the Spirit that he was the man called of God to bring peace and unity to the Ward. For the next ten years my father, as Bishop, did just that, and my mother helped him. She would have people from the ward over to dinner every Sunday. They befriended everyone: rich or poor, educated or uneducated, loving or petty and feuding with others. Systematically, they set an example of love and acceptance for everyone. My mother maintained a positive attitude while she assumed all of the household duties in order to free up my father, so that he could serve the people night after night."

"Wow. That's an amazing story. You really came from good parents," Sarah remarked. "But how do you know foreordination is a true principle?"

"The Book of Abraham sets a precedent for us in the scriptures, testifying of foreordination on earth. Foreordination means that we are called to a work in our pre-mortal life, but we have our free agency when we come to earth to discover what it is, and decide if we want to accomplish it. We can look at history and see that Christ was foreordained to a mission, as were Abraham, Moses, Joseph Smith, and an unknown like my father whose foreordination was foretold in his personal set of scriptures, his Patriarchal Blessing."

"Does everybody have a mission in life?"

"Yes, but it is up to us to find out what it is, develop our gifts and talents, and then fulfill it. We must always keep Christ's parable of the talents in mind. When we develop the talents and gifts that God has given us, they will be multiplied. Missions come in many forms, from giving birth to children, to noticing a child's talent and encouraging him or her to develop it, to a Father's loving support, to a volunteer's deeds of love, to writing a book, and on and on."

"Do we have only one mission?"

"We could define life as one overall mission, and within that mission are many parts or missions. For example, Christ's primary mission was to redeem mankind. He also had many other parts of his mission in creating, teaching, and helping others. We're all like that."

"Okay. I get it. But why are you talking so much about Patriarchal Blessings and foreordination?"

"Because that is what makes your marriage unique, and celestial bound. When I was single, in an LDS young adult group, one of the favorite topics to debate was: "Are we foreordained to marry only one specific person or could marriage to any one of a hundred different choices still be right?"

"Which one is right?" Sarah demanded to know.

"The fact is, both of these theories are correct. If a Patriarchal Blessing says that you were foreordained to marry a specific person, you are. Or if both of you have received personal revelation from the Lord that your spouse was foreordained for you, again the answer is obvious. Then again, there are some people on earth whose missions are very much like a hundred others so that they could conceivably marry a hundred different people and still fulfill the purposes of the Lord and the measure of their creation."

"That makes sense to me. But, sometimes I wonder if I should have married someone else!" Sarah lamented.

"Let me tell you about a unique movie that came out several years ago. The movie was called 'A Stranger Among Us.' It was a about a beautiful, worldly, woman detective who was assigned by the police department to investigate a murder mystery in a Chassidic Jewish community in New York City, a community that ran the diamond industry in midtown. Imagine movie star Melanie Griffith playing a woman detective. She is wearing a mini skirt and walks into the rabbi's Office where the Chassidic women are completely covered from their neck to wrists to ankles, and even their heads are covered with scarves or wigs. The contrast is heightened when worldly Melanie, who has to gain the confidence of these people, meets the rabbi's son. There is instant chemistry between them and they fall in love.

"One day at his school to become a rabbi, the rabbi's son is caught reading the Kabala by one of his fellow students. The friend tells him that he is not supposed to read those spiritual writings until he has mastered the Torah. The rabbi's son, spiritually ahead of his class, reads, 'The Kabala says that God counts a woman's tears.' He ponders out loud about how remarkable it is that God knows each of us so well and cares enough to even count a woman's tears. Later we see the rabbi's son telling Melanie about the Kabala. He explains to her the concept of a *besherta* and a *beshert*. In the Kabala, God teaches that there is one special person in the world created for each of us, a *beshert* (man) and a *besherta* (woman). We are destined to marry this person to fulfill our mission in life. The rabbi's son wants Melanie to be his *besherta*. He is tempted to run off with her. However, by a prearrangement, he is promised in marriage to the daughter of a French rabbi. She and her father are coming to New York in a week to meet the rabbi's son for the first time. In the climax of the show, Melanie gets shot while capturing the murderer. Now lying in a hospital bed, the rabbi's son cries, telling

Melanie that he cannot marry her because of his destiny to be a rabbi. The audience can see the torment in his face. Melanie cries. Then the hospital door opens and we see, the French rabbi and his daughter. She is beautiful and smart. She sees Melanie crying and says, 'Did you know that in the Kabala, it says that God counts a woman's tears.' Instantly the rabbi's son and the audience know that he has met his *besherta*. He has chosen correctly."

Sarah wiped a tear from her eye. "The great part of that story is the concept that God has one special person for you."

"Yes. Melanie would have prevented the rabbi's son from fulfilling his destiny as a rabbi. Only the French girl was prepared to help him accomplish his life's work. Likewise, God also loved Melanie Griffith's character. But she had a mission as a police detective. In fact she had just solved an impossible murder, performing a great service to the community. She needed a partner in life who would help her serve the public. At the end of the movie, she refuses to sleep with an old boyfriend and says, 'No, I'm waiting for my *beshert*.'"

"I wonder if I'm like that."

"Whether you feel you could have married ten righteous men in your life or not, now that you are married, you must decide to accept your chosen mate as your *beshert*. And from now on, determine that you have a mission together and that your mate is more important to you than anything or anyone else in the world."

"That's a tall order," Sarah whispered through her tears.

"Now is the beginning of the rest of your celestial marriage on earth. It is up to you to make it so."

"How can I do that?"

"This week, study out each other's Patriarchal Blessings. Outline your blessings into four categories: 1. Spiritual gifts and talents, 2. Potential missions, 3. Blessings and promises, and 4. Admonitions and advice. Then make out a plan of how you can support each other in fulfilling the missions you discover, using the gifts, talents, blessings, promises, admonitions and advice."

"Okay. I'm writing it down: spiritual gifts and blessings, potential missions, blessings and promises, and admonitions and advice."

"I remember so clearly when my husband was called to be a Bishop. So many people told me how sorry they were for me and offered condolences. I couldn't understand why. I was thrilled. It was the beginning of the fulfillment of one of my husband's missions in life. I was so happy and knew it was my calling too. Not that I would have anything to do with the running of the ward or confidential matters, but that I would serve my husband so that he could serve other people with joy, knowing I was behind him one hundred percent. I set out to have people over for dinner so he could become better acquainted with members of the ward. In this way, when he prayed to know whom he should call to certain positions in the ward, he could more easily receive revelations about the people and their needs. I saw to it that I took over the complete care of the children and household duties so that he was freed up. I never complained about him being gone. His success was my success. For years you have heard the cliché, 'A man is only as good as the woman behind him.' The reverse is also true. 'A woman is only as successful as the man who is behind her.'

"I never thought of it that way," Sarah said pensively.

"The Adam and Eve story is a model. We know that they were foreordained to a mission on earth. They supported each other. When Eve partook of the fruit, Adam could have said, 'You made a big mistake and you don't get to be with me anymore. Adios, babe! Nice knowing you!' But instead of judging her, he listened to her. He didn't yell. He analyzed the situation. Then, he realized that they had a mission together, multiplying and replenishing the earth. He knew that he must support his wife in her decision. She had made the right choice to further their progression on earth, and he followed. It is a wonderful story of oneness and deciding to serve a mission together.

"Studying your spouse's Patriarchal Blessing is about support. In fact, the hallmark of a celestial marriage should be support, with the vision and the ability to always see the entire picture, the big picture."

"I think I'm really getting it now. A celestial love is the opposite of being small minded and myopic. It is about seeing your husband or wife as the Lord sees them," Sarah exclaimed, proud of herself.

"A celestial marriage never criticizes. A celestial marriage provides an environment for growth and potential. Today I am asking you to capture the vision of your life together. And then treat each other as the celebrities you are. Wouldn't you treat your husband differently if you thought he was going to become a prophet of the Lord?"

"No kidding, or the man who was voted the most influential high school teacher of the year, which he was."

"That's terrific. You're getting it. And I bet your husband would treat you differently if he thought you had a special mission to your daughter Lily, a mission given to you by your Heavenly Father. Even more important is the knowledge that you are married to a potential future god. And you have the potential to become a goddess of another world."

"That really is profound."

"You bet it is. I have seen good men and women passed over for advancement in the world because their mates are like a millstone around their neck. Ask yourself this question: Are you a builder of your spouse or a destroyer of his human spirit?"

"Eeek! I'm afraid I criticize my husband a lot. He irritates me so often."

"When growing up, I never heard my father criticize me. He seemed to look for opportunities to praise me and build my self-esteem. If I made a mistake he would take a philosophical approach, asking me what I had learned from that experience. Somehow this question made me feel good about myself as I'd recount the dreadful experience. He'd always listen intently. Finally I'd tell him what I had learned and how I'd do it all over again differently. His eyes would sparkle and then well up with tears of love. Regaining his composure he'd say, 'Oh Laura, I am so proud of you. What great wisdom the Lord has given you.' My heart would soar. I'd leave his presence wanting to be a better person, wanting to succeed for him so that he'd always be proud of me."

"I wish that I had had a father like that. Maybe I wouldn't be so critical of my husband."

"In contrast to my loving father was the father of one of my friends named Sol. He never once heard his father tell him that he loved him. Sol's father was critical of him and everyone else. If he ever had a new idea, his father would sabotage it or tell him, 'I had no idea you were so far gone,' or, 'How can you be so stupid?' My friend learned to do things in secret. He achieved remarkable success, despite the negative influence. As an adult, Sol learned to never ask his father's opinion or advice because it would always be negative. His father claimed to be one of the great minds of the world and yet he failed to understand human nature. Sol's father was a destroyer of the human spirit. However, if interviewed, he would say that criticism was good. The difference between Sol and me was a word called 'self-esteem.' My father instilled in me a confidence that I could accomplish anything. Of course, he gave me advice if I asked for it. After all, he was my parental mentor. On the heels of his advice, he would make me feel that I was important to the Lord, and that I would accomplish a special mission on earth. Sol's father filled his mind with self-doubts and a pursuit for approval from others. Sol was brilliant and far more capable in many areas than others, and yet he would almost always defer to others' authority. Subconsciously, he was still trying to win the approval and love of his father.

"Sol overcame his environment due to a loving, supportive wife who saw his potential. She saw him through the eyes of the Lord, focusing on his gifts and talents. She made it one of her missions to help him achieve his dreams, goals, and missions in life. He married a builder of people, not a destroyer of the human spirit."

"That is a great example of a woman who made it her mission to help her husband."

"Yes, it is. Over the years, I have seen couples who were once madly in love deteriorate to the level of destroyers of each other. It is shameful to see the negativity that crept into their marriages, and how it stifled their individual growth and their growth together as a couple. What potential they had! What great things they could have achieved! Instead, they ended up like two hostile enemies co-habitating, and some eventually divorced.

"A celestial couple constantly revisits the vision the Lord has in their Patriarchal Blessings. They know that whether their missions in life are spiritual or secular, recognized by millions of people or known only by each other, they are equally important to the Lord. There should not be any difference between our secular lives and our spiritual lives, for all things are spiritual unto the Lord."

"What do you mean?" asked Sarah.

"Let me give you an example. I almost married another man. In fact, it was only two weeks before the wedding that we called it off. We were simply not meant to be together. The Lord loved us both so much that He knew that neither one of us could be married to each other and accomplish the missions that the Lord had in store for us. We parted friends, so we could find our eternal mates. He became a Bishop just like my husband. He was a good man, but he was not the man for me. Part of his secular mission was to have six children. That was not my mission. I was limited to two children, one by natural childbirth and one by adoption. His Patriarchal Blessing emphasized his mission to his children. Mine emphasized teaching principles of the gospel to the young and rising generation. He chose a different career field than my husband's and mine. I wouldn't have had the opportunities to fulfill my mission on earth. For example, my husband and I founded a television production business. I had a show on TV for four years called *Teens Talk*. It aired nationally on a cable network. In this show, I was able to influence teenagers for good by addressing vital topics of the day, and even planting seeds of the gospel. It was the merging of my secular and spiritual missions and could have only happened with my husband, Conrad, my *beshert*.

"One show featured an 18-year-old Christian girl who requested the opportunity to appear on *Teens Talk* to debate the issue of abortion.

She was magnificent. As she debated the pro-choice advocate, she talked about consequences of our actions and taking responsibility for the choices we make in life. She asked the TV audience, 'How many of you think that it would be wrong to get an abortion if you were a couple of months pregnant, going to Hawaii in three months, and didn't want to look fat in your bikini?' The camera turned on the audience and everyone raised their hand, indicating that they thought it was wrong in that case. She then said, 'See, you attach importance to the fetus. That means, deep down inside, you believe that abortion is wrong.' She was powerful.

"I also had a show with unwed teen mothers. They told about how they were going to adopt their babies out, and advised other pregnant teens to do the same for the sake of their own development and for the sake of the children who deserved to have both a mother and a father ready to nurture a family. Another show entitled, 'The Last Two Virgins in High School', focused on the benefits of sexual purity and how to say 'no' to sex before marriage.

"If I did nothing else in my life on earth, I know that I had a mission to make those shows, and many others which advocated correct principles. This mission was both secular and spiritual, and that's what I mean when I say that there should be no difference between the two. If I only helped one person find spiritual truth through my secular efforts, it was worth it."

"And now, you're helping me save my marriage," Sarah offered.

"I'm glad you feel that way," I continued. "A celestial marriage isn't selfish. It focuses on teamwork. It centers on owning each other's missions and dreams in life to literally fulfill the measure of each other's creation."

"What if a person doesn't feel like they have a mission, or they can't seem to really see anything specific in their Patriarchal Blessing?"

"This is not unique. Maybe it isn't time for you to understand exactly what missions lie ahead. Even Christ did not have a sure witness of what his mission was in life until he fasted for forty days in the desert. Then He learned that He truly was the Only Begotten in the flesh and the literal second member of the Godhead. He learned of his missions: to teach us the way to return to our Heavenly Father, and to atone for our sins that we might be forgiven and receive eternal life.

"As he was growing up, Jesus learned what his gifts and talents were. When he was teaching in the temple at age twelve he received a glimpse that He had a gift and a mission beyond that of any mortal man.

"We will receive glimpses of our talents from our Patriarchal Blessing, from learning from other people like our mother or father, brother or sister, or friends, and from success in school or in our various activities. We can learn of them through prayer or reading in the scriptures. The Holy Ghost can whisper to us at any time in the spirit of personal revelation. What matters is that we develop our gifts and talents along the way, and commit to supporting our mates in developing theirs."

Sarah opened her scriptures to Section 46 of the Doctrine and Covenants. "This is the section on Spiritual gifts," she said.

"Hey, you're good! You've been studying your scriptures. Go ahead and read verses 11 through 30 out loud."

For all have not every gift given unto them; for there are many gifts, and to every man is given a gift by the Spirit of God.

To some is given one, and to some is given, another, that all may be profited thereby.

To some it is given by the Holy Ghost to know that Jesus Christ is the Son of God, and that he was crucified for the sins of the world.

To others it is given to believe on their words, that they also might have eternal life if they continue faithful.

And again, to some it is given by the Holy Ghost to know the differences of administration, as it will be pleasing unto the same Lord, according as the Lord will, suiting his mercies, according to the conditions of the children of men.

And again, it is given by the Holy Ghost to some to know the diversities of operations, whether they be of God, that the manifestations of the Spirit may be given to every man to profit withal.

And again, verily I say unto you, to some is given, by the Spirit of God, the word of wisdom.

To another is given the word of knowledge, that all may be taught to be wise and to have knowledge.

And again, to some it is given to have faith to be healed;

And to others it is given to have faith to heal.

And again, to some is given the working of miracles;

And to others it is given to prophesy;

And to others the discerning of spirits.

And again, it is given to some to speak with tongues;

And to another is given the interpretation of tongues.

And all these gifts come from God, for the benefit of the children of God.

And unto the Bishop of the church, and unto such as God shall appoint and ordain to watch over the church and to be elders unto the church, are to have it given unto them to discern all those gifts lest there shall be any among you professing and yet be not of God.

And it shall come to pass that he that asketh in Spirit shall receive in Spirit; That unto some it may be given to have all those gifts, that there may be a head, in order that every member may be profited thereby.

He that asketh in the Spirit asketh according to the will of God; wherefore it is done even as he asketh.

"Thank you, Sarah. Part of developing our gifts is magnifying the free agency on earth that Heavenly Father entrusted us with. Moses, Abraham, Joseph Smith, Lyman Nielson (my father), Mary (mother of Jesus), Esther, and many others, all had to develop their gifts and decide to follow the Lord and accept the missions they were called to do. Some missions in life may not seem spectacular, make us famous, or make us rich. But, our missions can fulfill our destinies and lead us back to Heavenly Father. What could be more important?

"It is sad when a person is called by the authority of God, through an inspired Bishop, and a spouse puts pressure on him or her to turn it down. This happens when one mate does not have a clear vision of their life together or a desire to support a spouse to fulfill the measure of his or her creation. Such a decision can alter the entire destiny of an individual. Support for a mate can be sacrificial and difficult, but the joy of seeing your wife or husband accomplish the purposes of the Lord brings incredible unity.

"An acquaintance of mine married a man she converted to the Church of Jesus Christ of Latter-Day Saints. He was a choice man who had looked for the truth all his life. He had natural leadership skills and their potential together was obvious. Sadly, after a few years, it became apparent that they didn't have an overall vision of their missions together or separately. One day the Bishop of their ward was inspired to call the man to be the Young Men's President. Unfortunately, the man turned it down. Subsequently they found other activities to fill their lives and both became inactive in church. My heart cried out for them, and this missed opportunity and mission to serve others even as Christ did.

"I wish that every spouse on earth could have a vision of the great potential of their mate. I wish that every man and woman would love their sweetheart so much that they would put them first, that they would do everything in their power to support their mate's development on earth. Isn't that what perfection is all about?"

"I never thought of it that way before. I can't wait to read our blessings together," Sarah remarked with enthusiasm.

"When you see each other through the Lord's eyes, you will want to spend the rest of your lives striving for perfection, supporting each other, and increasing your spiritual gifts and talents."

"I get so tied up and bogged down managing our home, taking care of the children, with the volunteer work I do in the community, my church service, and taking care of the needs of my husband. It's no wonder we always end up in a fight," Sarah lamented.

"You're not unusual. With so much to do, tempers can flare when a mate falls through on a promise or disappoints us in some way."

"That's it. That's what happens to us. I criticize Jake and he criticizes me for falling through on promises."

"It's times like this that the lofty dreams and visions of each other's greatness fade from view."

"Fade from view? They're blasted to smithereens!"

Sarah and I burst into laughter. I continued, "One time I was so angry with my husband that I began to mentally process memories of all the other boyfriends I could have married. I was in a martyr-like state of mind. I can't remember what it was that my husband did to enrage me now. It's long been forgotten. But what stands out vividly in my mind is the spiritual experience that occurred on this occasion. Suddenly the words flowed through my mind, 'If you only knew who he was!' This message from the Holy Spirit was distinct and powerful. In fact it completely stunned me and took me aback. I remember flopping down on my bed and thinking how petty I had been. I thought about what had touched me off and realized that it wouldn't mean a thing in the eternities of time. I reviewed my husband's great qualities. I thought about the hopes, dreams, and goals that we had made together, both long term and short term. I got caught up in our mission together, my husband's mission and my mission on earth. Then, I thought about the times I had hurt my husband, and how he had always forgiven me. Could I do any less? After all, none of us are perfect."

"You make me feel ashamed of myself. I've been so hard on my husband."

"And he on you?"

"Yes."

"Now I always use the expression, 'This won't matter in the eternities of time,' to get me out of the unimportant, and back on the celestial track of seeing my husband through God's eyes. I know that whatever incident is bothering me now will not matter in the eternities of time. But my mission, his mission, and our missions will. This is the foundation of a celestial marriage. Always see your mate through the

Lord's eyes and always do everything in your power to support your mate in achieving his or her mission on earth."

Just then, we heard cries coming from Sarah's playroom followed by two little girls with scraped knees hobbling out into the living room. We laughed quietly, and marveled at the perfect timing. I left with a promise to return and gave her the second assignment for achieving a successful celestial marriage on earth.

ASSIGNMENT NUMBER TWO:

1. Read each other's Patriarchal Blessings out loud to each other.
2. Outline each according to the following:

   ◆ Spiritual gifts and talents
   ◆ Potential missions
   ◆ Blessings and promises
   ◆ Admonitions and advice

3. Write: how you will help and support your spouse achieve his or her mission on earth.
4. Write: how you will help your spouse develop his or her spiritual gifts and talents associated with his or her mission in life.
5. Write out things you can do to live up to the admonitions and advice.

CHAPTER 3

PROBLEM SOLVING
AND DECISION MAKING

The red brick Tudor house seemed to glow in the setting sun. The hot pink rhododendron blossoms were bursting forth in full bloom. The carved oak door flung open as Sarah jubilantly pointed to her eager husband.

"Do you mind me sitting in on your session today?" he pleaded. "These last two weeks of living the 'Five Pillars of a Celestial Marriage' have brought us closer together. And then when we read our Patriarchal Blessings and realized just who we were married to, you know - the way the Lord sees our mate, well it's changed our lives. We've never been happier. So..."

I interrupted to set him at ease. "Of course. I'm delighted to teach you together."

My captive audience led me to their old English dining room set, seated me politely in one of their antique Elizabethan chairs, pulled out their notebooks and readied themselves for serious note taking. My attention was diverted momentarily as an ornate grandfather's clock chimed seven times. I only had one hour before honoring my daughter Elisabeth's bedtime, complete with story and prayer. I plunged forward into my lecture.

"Twenty years ago, six young couples made their wedding vows in an LDS Temple, a House of the Lord, where they were married for time and all eternity. They were all filled with hopes and dreams. In fact, they were all convinced that no one had been in love like they were. They felt that they would never fight, never have problems, and never divorce because theirs was the perfect love. Now, all these years later, only three of the six couples are still married."

"What went wrong?" they asked simultaneously.

"We could point our finger at the financial difficulties of one of the couples, or the adultery of another, or the growing in two different directions in the third. But these would only be the outward symptoms of the underlying problem in each of the three cases. What ruined these marriages? I believe it was because none of them learned how to make decisions together as a couple. None of them learned how to solve problems together as a team."

"It's hard. That's one of the reasons we end up fighting with each other," Jake offered.

"Unfortunately, your situation is not uncommon. When we are baptized members of the Church of Jesus Christ of Latter-Day Saints, we are given the gift of the Holy Ghost. This third member of the Godhead is to be our constant guide and companion, to lead us into the paths of righteousness and inspire us when we need help."

"What does that have to do with problem solving as a couple?" Sarah asked with genuine interest.

"When I married, I knew that we had to make decisions together. We needed guidance in our lives as a married couple, not as two separate entities who just happened to be living together. Knowing that God was a third partner in our marriage, I knew we could not fail as a team if we always consulted Him in couple's prayers. But, before a couple can receive answers from the Holy Spirit together, they must first know and understand how to receive personal revelation. All of my life I have made it my mission to learn how to receive personal revelation through the Gift of the Holy Spirit in making decisions."

"That makes sense," Sarah added.

"When I was serving a full-time mission in Northern France, I clearly remember attending a special missionary conference in Nantes. I can still envision President Smith B. Griffin delivering a talk that would change my life forever. He said, 'You are here to learn to develop an automatic problem solving mechanism within yourself.' His words are indelible in my memory. President Griffin's philosophy was that each of us had to learn how to solve our own problems, and that the ability to do so would ultimately determine the level of success we would achieve in our lives.

"Some people wallow in the same problems year after year, never changing in any way, and never trying to come up with an answer or a solution. They seem to like to complain. What differentiates any human from another is the ability to solve problems and to move on to greater things. Those who wallow in self-pity stifle their growth and ability to accomplish what they want in life."

"I'm ashamed to admit that I've always had trouble making decisions by myself, let alone as a couple," Jake admitted.

"Section 9 of the *Doctrine and Covenants* gives us the blueprint on how we can make decisions as a couple and solve problems. Here is the background story of the revelation. Oliver Cowdery wanted to translate the Gold Plates rather than just be the scribe. On several occasions he asked Joseph if he could be a translator, too. Softhearted, Joseph inquired of the Lord to see if it was okay for Oliver to try. The Prophet felt inspired from the Holy Spirit to let Oliver have a go at translating. But, when Oliver Cowdery was unable to figure out what the characters meant, he was terribly disappointed. It was at this time that Joseph Smith received the famous revelation recorded in section 9. Verses 8 and 9 say: 'But, behold, I say unto you, that you must study it out in your mind; then you must ask me if it be right, and if it is right I will cause that your bosom shall burn within you; therefore, you shall feel that it is right.

"'But if it be not right you shall have no such feelings, but you shall have a stupor of thought that shall cause you to forget the thing which is wrong; therefore, you cannot write that which is sacred save it be given you from me.'

"I love this revelation. I often times think that if I could only have the benefit of one scripture, one revelation, I would choose this one because it tells us clearly how to receive answers to our prayers from the Lord. And if we know how to receive personal revelation we can solve all of our problems.

"First, we must study out the problem that is bothering us. We must weigh the pros and cons of each possible solution, and then decide which answer appears to be the right one. This solution is based on our own study, wisdom, and discernment. Then, we are to ask God if that is truly the right answer. In D&C 9:8-9, God clearly tells us that we will know if our answer is right by the feeling He gives us in our heart. It could be a euphoric feeling, a peaceful feeling, a feeling of a swelling in our heart which I describe as a 'whoosh' feeling, or just a calm feeling of knowing that it is right. But, on the other hand, if it is wrong, we will feel confused. One minute we might think that it is right and the next minute we will feel it is wrong, or we might just feel depressed. That means the answer is 'no' and we must try another solution to our problem.

"Ninety-nine percent of the time the Lord answers our prayers in these ways. That is why He gives us the gift of the Holy Ghost when we are so young. We receive this gift at age eight to guide us early in our lives. The sooner we can master the knowledge and feelings of how the Spirit reveals answers to our prayers, the sooner we can avoid most of the pitfalls of life."

Jake looked frustrated. "What are you thinking, Jake?" I asked. "I feel as if I've lost you somewhere."

"No. I understand the principle. But it's what you were saying about mastering how the Spirit reveals answers to our prayers. I feel totally stupid that I'm a returned missionary, and I still don't really know how or when the Spirit is talking to me. Often I think it's my own feelings or emotions taking over," Jake practically whispered, embarrassed by his admission.

"Let me give you an example," I continued. "A young woman named Coral was devastated by the accidental death of her husband. She suffered greatly going through a difficult grieving process. A year later, while skiing, she met a handsome Mormon named John, a man who would change her life forever. Coincidentally, John's wife had passed away six months prior to their encounter. They were both in their early 40's, and drawn to each other through their sorrow. As their relationship continued, they began dating formally and fell in love. It seemed that divine intervention brought them together. Coral soon joined the church and they were married in the temple.

"As time passed and the initial excitement of marriage wore off, John's children had trouble accepting their new mother, and began causing her an immense amount of emotional pain. The in-laws began to find fault, too. Life took a turn for Coral and the vicissitudes of life took their toll. Holiday parties tended to be miserable experiences for her. As another Thanksgiving rolled around, she announced to John that she didn't want to spend another holiday filled with contention, his disrespectful children, and the in-laws. On the other hand, she loved John and hated to let him down. The couple didn't know what to do, so they went to their stake president for counseling. He told them to go home and pray about it.

"This is where I come in. I was writing an article for *OnLine Magazine*, a publication we printed for the film and video community of the Pacific Northwest. For some reason, I felt inspired to interrupt my editing and call Coral to ask her how she was doing. Her voice cracked, and it sounded like she was choking back tears. I asked what was wrong, and she readily confided her dilemma to me. I responded, 'How have you been praying?' She said, 'I've been asking the Lord if I should go to the Thanksgiving dinner at my in-laws or not. And I just don't seem to get an answer.' 'That's your problem', I exclaimed as if I were Sherlock Holmes solving the crime of the century. 'You must first study it out in your mind, decide on an answer, and then ask the Lord if it is right. If you feel depressed about it or cry a lot, or are irritable, unhappy, etcetera, then it is wrong and you should try again. Since you don't want to go, try first saying to the Lord that you've decided not to go, and ask Him if that is right. If not, ask the reverse.'"

"She said 'okay' and got off the phone. I'm used to people not taking my advice, so I didn't expect to hear about it again. To my surprise, Coral called me the next day and told me that she had had the most profound spiritual experience of her entire life. Coral said that she knelt down on her knees right after we had talked, and asked the Lord if it was right that she had decided not to go to the Thanksgiving dinner. She started crying. She thought to herself, 'Oh, I'm just being emotional. I'll wait a few hours and see if I feel peaceful.' Unhappily, she continued to cry for two hours and couldn't stop.

"Finally, she said to herself, 'This must be what Laura was talking about. All this crying must mean 'no.' So, she got back down on her knees and prayed to the Lord saying, 'I've decided to go with my husband to the Thanksgiving party regardless of the fact that they always hurt me. I'll go just to support my husband and have faith that I'm supposed to be there. If this is right bless me with a peaceful feeling.' She stopped crying immediately. The contrast was so immediate and dramatic, she was stunned. Then a peaceful feeling came over her, and she absolutely knew, without a doubt, that she had an answer from the Lord.

"She told me that she couldn't believe she had never been taught this wonderful way to receive answers to her prayers. Now Coral and John are firm believers in solving their problems together using prayer. When we turn to the Lord, our third partner in our marriage, we will always receive answers to our prayers to help us make the right decisions. The bonus from making decisions together is incredible unity, and the development of a celestial marriage on earth."

"Forgive me if I appear a little slow here," Jake confessed. "I get the idea that answers from the Lord create unity in a marriage. Believe me– we want that. Don't we, Sarah?"

"Yeah," Sarah affirmed.

"But, I don't cry when the Lord's trying to tell me 'no'!" Jake blurted out.

I couldn't help myself and began laughing. I couldn't picture this husky guy crying at any time! "Pardon me, Jake, I didn't mean to imply by this story that everyone who receives a 'no' answer from the Lord will begin an uncontrollable crying fit. Remember in D&C 9:8-9, it said that if it isn't right the Lord will cause you to have a stupor of thought?"

"Yeah, so?"

"Well, for me a stupor of thought is like depression. And to some people, depression is like crying. To others it's an irritable attitude for awhile. To yet others they just simply forget that they were asking for something. Then, there are many variations in between. We all have to learn how to listen to the Holy Spirit in our own way and then master it."

Jake and Sarah shrugged their shoulders and flopped back in their chairs as if they were ready to give up before they started.

"Let me tell you a story of learning the hard way how to listen to the Spirit of the Holy Ghost. In 1973 I was engaged to a wonderful man whom I will refer to as Ken. Ken and I felt very close to each other spiritually. We would often say we were spiritual twins. We had grown up together. My father had baptized us both on the same day at age eight. In short, we knew each other well, and loved and respected each other. He was ambitious and working on his MBA at Brigham Young University. However, there was a snag in our plans. Every time I prayed to know if I should marry Ken, I felt depressed.

"I was twenty-four years old and still a novice at recognizing answers to my prayers. I kept reviewing in my mind all of his wonderful qualities. He was intelligent, ambitious, tender hearted, had pure faith, and was what I call a 'spiritual giant.' I had always wanted to marry someone just like my father, spiritual in every way, and truly dedicated to the Lord. Ken had all of these qualities.

"I knew that who I married was the most important decision I would ever make in my life. I wanted approval from the Lord that I was making the right decision. I went through endless days of confusion of thought. Although I knew that my answer would be given to me by the power of the Holy Ghost, I wasn't able to discern the answer that was coming to me. I have a great testimony that if we are sincere in heart, truly keeping the Lord's commandments, and want to do what is right, the Lord has tender mercy upon our souls and will help us recognize the answer in another way.

"As yet, I hadn't recognized that a depression or confusion of thought was a 'no' answer from the Lord. All of my previous prayers had just been answered directly by giving me exactly what I had asked for. My head was too clouded to hear the answer. I was filled with a confusion of thought. One day I believed I should marry Ken, and the next I thought that I shouldn't. I was so confused. At work I was depressed. I just wasn't happy and wondered why.

"Finally, I fasted and prayed to know if I should marry Ken. Afterwards, I was irritable all day long and confused. My parents were so patient. I had already had two wedding shower parties. My wedding dress was ready. Five hundred engraved wedding invitations were all addressed, and ready to mail. They remained on my mother's desk pending my decision to marry. Each day my mother would ask me if I had made up my mind.

"Finally, only two weeks before the wedding, my mother kindly pointed out to me the urgency of my decision. We were already socially out of sync by not sending out the wedding reception invitations at least one month in advance. My parents advised me to fly down to Utah, visit Ken, and decide once and for all if he was the one the Lord wanted me to marry.

"When I arrived in Provo, I told Ken how I felt. He listened with loving understanding. He knew that I loved him, but he wanted what the Lord desired for each of us. We decided to go to the temple fasting and praying to know what we should do. I went through an endowment session and he went to the baptistry where he was an ordinance worker. During the entire endowment service I kept crying. I remember pleading with the Lord to give me the answer. Was I making the right decision to marry Ken? The more I asked, the more I sobbed. The more I cried, the more confused I felt. The confusion swarmed around me like a thousand yellow jackets threatening to sting me. The result was intense anxiety.

"Finally, I said, 'Father in Heaven, please forgive me, but I just can't hear the answer.' Then, I asked him to show me a sign if I was supposed to marry Ken. I asked the Lord to have my fiancé waiting for me in the lobby when I was finished with the endowment service. That would be the sign that Ken was the one the Lord wanted me to marry. On the other hand, if Ken was not present when I arrived in the lobby, I would know that he was not my eternal mate."

"He wasn't in the lobby waiting for you, right?"

"You guessed it. But did I know then that he wasn't the one? Did I know that this was a sign that came from the Lord who had such mercy on me? No, I didn't. I was still so emotional. I prayed, 'Oh Father in Heaven, I know I'm not supposed to ask for signs, so maybe I was being unrighteous when I asked for one and this isn't the answer.'"

"Yikes! Were you clueless or what?" Sarah laughed.

"I was clueless alright. I was so caught up in the fact that I could only get married once, and that I had to marry the one the Lord wanted for me. I was so intensely filled with my own emotions, I just couldn't hear the answer."

"That's my problem," Jake interjected. "So what did you do?"

"Well, this is what happened next. I prayed saying, 'Father in Heaven, forgive me, but if I'm not supposed to marry Ken, you've just got to have him call off the wedding.' Sure enough, when he came out of the baptistry, he said, 'Let's call off the wedding. You move down here right away, and we'll continue our courtship and decide later if we should marry.' He called off the wedding! That was my answer. I knew that we were not meant to marry each other. A peace came over me and filled my whole being with an immediate calm. It was a dramatic contrast to the confusion, depression, crying, and irritable feelings I had experienced over the past six months. Now I absolutely knew the Lord had answered my prayers.

"Over the next week, I analyzed what had happened. The Lord had cared about me so much that he had tried several ways to answer my prayers. I realized what tender loving mercy the Lord has for each one of us. It reminded me of when I was the only freshman taking geometry in my High School. Algebra had been a snap. But geometry was an entirely different story. I would try so hard to understand the teacher's explanations in class. But, I just couldn't understand what he was saying. I'd come home from school and have my father help me. I'd cry and cry and say, 'I just don't get it.' My patient, ever-so-loving father would then invent another system of teaching me until the light bulb went on in my head. The next day I'd go to school and earn 100% on the pop quiz. I don't remember ever getting anything lower than 100% on a test, thanks to my father's understanding, love, and patience. My father wanted to help me because I was trying so hard to be a success. This is exactly how Father in Heaven feels about us. If we are trying to receive an answer to our prayers from Him, he will do everything He can to give us that answer, even as my earthly father did for me in geometry, my freshman year in high school.

"Breaking off my engagement and receiving an answer to my prayers was one of the all-time great lessons of my life. From this experience I clearly knew how to discern a 'no' answer to prayer. I have thanked my Father in Heaven many times over for teaching me that valuable lesson. And I have always been grateful to Ken for his spirituality and mutual knowing that we were not meant to marry each other. Twenty-five years later I can clearly see that the Lord had specific missions for each of us that could not be accomplished together. How blessed I was to learn this lesson with an eternal and valued friend!

"My engagement story dramatically illustrates two points. One, it defines clearly how we can receive answers to our prayers through the gift of the Holy Spirit. If we feel depressed or have a confusion of thought, it is a 'no' from the Lord. If we feel peaceful and no longer waiver in the decision, it means 'yes' from the Lord. Secondly, this story indicates that the Lord has great understanding for us during the learning curve. He wants to get through to us with the answer when we are sincerely asking. So, often He will answer the prayer in more than one way. If we don't recognize the first Holy Ghost witness, He will keep sending it until we do, or He will send a second witness through another means."

Sarah sat up straight and glared at me. "This is all well and good, but you clearly said that we have to receive answers from the Lord as a couple and no longer as individuals to the problems and decisions in our marriage? So how do we do that?"

"You are absolutely right. Major decisions must be made together in order to achieve harmony, unity, and a deeper love for one another. But, some partners I've taught in my class have believed that they can and should make decisions for the marriage by themselves. Some men assume that a decision about their job is solely their responsibility. It doesn't occur to them that they should consult their wife about accepting a job offer or making a career change. Why do you think that this assumption is dangerous? Why would it potentially drive a wedge into the oneness of a marriage?"

Jake answered. "Well, if I accepted a job in California, and we had to move, it would affect Sarah and the kids. Sarah would lose the friendships she's had our whole married life. Sarah wouldn't be living near her parents anymore. Plus, right now, she is the Merrie Miss advisor, and everyone says the girls respond so well to her. She even reactivated one girl. I think that she is serving a kind of mission with the girls. Our children would be affected by the move too. It could be that a move would be wrong for the children. Maybe they'd end up in schools that were undesirable."

"Good. You see how a decision in regards to where you work is just as important to your wife and children's future as it is to yours. You'd be surprised to hear how many men think that this is a decision for the patriarch of the family to make. Unfortunately they misunderstand the function of a real patriarch: one who makes decisions *with* his wife, not *for* her. Besides, to independently pray about a job opportunity, without a spouse's input, is contrary to the establishment of nightly couple's prayer, during which time both of you consult the Lord regarding your lives together. When a couple has already established a pattern of praying together nightly, holding hands, and envisioning themselves kneeling in the presence of the Lord, it is unthinkable to suddenly make a decision alone. As my daughter would say: 'Hello!' In teen lingo this means, 'You still don't get it, do you?'

"A husband who doesn't consult his wife about moving is

inconsiderate, besides the fact that he is not taking advantage of his partnership, another opinion, and another witness to an answer from the Lord. If you believe that it matters where you live because it makes a difference where you will be able to accomplish the mission the Lord has in store for you, then you must pray about it together.

"I remember my parents praying together to know if my father should take a job in Oregon. They both had an overwhelming Holy Ghost feeling in their hearts that the move was right. Remember, I told you about my father's great mission in the Puget Sound area? In Oregon, it was my mother's turn. Within a short time of moving, my mother was called to be the Stake Young Women's President. She was a creative and visionary woman. She saw a need for the church to have its own campground for Girls Camp and Boy Scouts Camp. She prayed about it and felt that she was inspired by the Lord to propose the idea to the Stake. When she told the Stake Presidency, they felt the Spirit of the Lord and agreed that it was meant to be. The Stake President received permission from Church headquarters, and a search for a site began. My father supported my mother by driving her all over the valley in search of the property the Lord wanted them to purchase. The rest is history. With the help of others, they found a prime piece of property, received permission from Church headquarters to purchase it, and since then many generations of children have enjoyed the campgrounds."

"That story makes me cry because we all want to feel that we can make a difference in the world," Sarah added.

"Exactly. And you are too, Sarah. You've already changed a young girl's life by reactivating her. By bringing her back into the fold, you may have saved her from going on drugs, getting pregnant out of wedlock, or any number of life's disasters.

"A celestial marriage takes into consideration the talents and missions of both partners. A celestial marriage makes decisions together with the help of a third partner, the Lord. Now that we've established the importance of making decisions together..."

Sarah interrupted. "We get it already. I want to know how to receive answers to our prayers as a couple."

"I'm sorry," I apologized. "Sometimes I get carried away. Okay. How do you receive answers to your prayers as a couple?" I actually wrote them out for you." I handed Jake and Sarah each a copy of my handout.

HOW TO RECEIVE ANSWERS
TO YOUR PRAYERS AS A COUPLE

1. Both partners should have an open mind and display an attitude of humility. They know that whatever the answer is from the Lord, both partners are ultimately winners because the Lord wants what is best for both and knows the future.

2. Study out the problem together, with all of the necessary facts.

3. List the pros and cons for each potential decision.

4. Make a decision based on the knowledge you have gathered. What makes the best sense? Maybe the husband sides with the cons and the wife sides with the pros. In this situation, one partner must politely give up his/her view and be willing to see if the partner's decision is the right one. They know that if their mate's decision is right, they are not the loser. They will be a winner because the Lord knows what's right for both.

5. Then, take the decision to the Lord and ask Him if it is right.

6. Wait to see what feelings each partner receives. If one feels good about a decision and the other one feels badly, it is a 'no' answer from the Lord. You both must receive a good feeling for it to be a 'yes' answer.

7. If the answer is 'no,' with a confusion of thought, depression, incessant tears, irritability, or one spouse feels good about the decision and the other spouse feels negative, then go back to the beginning. Make another decision and take it to the Lord, repeating the same prayer process.

"You are repeating the same steps for receiving answers to your prayers as a single person." Jake interjected impatiently. "But, you said that Sarah and I have to receive the same answer for it to be right, and yet, if it is 'no,' one of us could have received a 'yes' answer. That is very confusing to me. Please explain again what you mean."

"If the decision is 'yes' from the Lord you will both:

1. Feel peaceful.

2. Feel good.

3. Feel euphoric, a swelling in the heart, or what I call a 'whoosh' feeling.

4. Have a knowing feeling that it is right.

5. Feel no wavering of thought, only a constant feeling of it being right.
6. Have a thought run quickly through your mind such as, 'It's right. Take the job.'

"If one feels good and the other feels peaceful, it is a 'yes.' You both just have a different way of receiving a 'yes' from the Holy Spirit. However, if one of you feels good, and the other feels depressed, it is a 'no' answer from the Lord."

"Couldn't one of us be in tune and the other one have received the wrong answer from the Lord?" Jake queried.

"If you both are sincerely trying to receive the answer from the Lord with an open mind, this process, with practice, will always work. If one receives a 'yes' answer and the other one receives a 'no' answer via depression or stupor of thought, it is clearly a 'no' answer from the Lord."

"Why? I still don't get it."

"Because the answer has come as a confusion of thought between the two of you. A 'yes' answer for a couple will always be felt by both of you.

"A 'no' answer from the Lord can come to each of you in one of the following ways:

1. A depressed feeling.
2. Angry, upset, or irritable feelings with no explainable reason.
3. Confusion of thought. A 'yes' feeling one day and a 'no' feeling the next, and so it continues every day or hour, a different feeling. That is a confusion of thought.
4. Constantly crying or emotional outbursts of negativity with no explainable reason.

"Maybe this is clear to you. But, I really have trouble understanding this principle. Could you give us some examples," Jake pleaded.

"Sure. Eleven years ago I wanted to buy a house. We lived in a small apartment. Our son slept in a closet and the apartment was upstairs from the business. All of my friends had long since bought lovely houses in the suburbs and were doing great. We had started a business, instead of buying a house. After five years, we were starting to make money and I thought it was a good time to buy. My husband, Conrad, thought that it wasn't the right time. But, rather than saying 'no' right away, he was humble and said, 'Okay, I could be mistaken. Let's study it out and make a decision, pray about it, and if it's right, we'll do it.' I remember hugging him, I was so excited about the possibility.

"We studied our finances and figured out what we could afford and how we'd scrape by making the payments. Conrad still did not want to buy a house at the time, but was open to what the Lord wanted for us. Next we went house shopping. It was so much fun. At last my dreams were coming true. We found a house for the right price, and put section 9 of the *Doctrine and Covenants* to a test. We prayed and asked Father in Heaven to bless us with a good feeling if we had made the right decision to buy the house. And, if it was wrong, we asked Him to bless us that we would have a depression of thought. We knew that God knew our future, and we wanted to make the right decision.

"That Sunday we visited the new ward we would attend, if we bought the house. We only had time to spend ten minutes in the Relief Society and Priesthood because of our callings in our regular ward. But, ten minutes was all that we needed. When we met in the car, we compared notes. We both had extremely depressing feelings about buying the house at that time. We knew that was the answer from the Lord. We needed to keep our cash in the business at that time and weren't ready to buy. Now, I could have looked at the problem as if I was the loser. I didn't get the house that I wanted. Conrad was the 'winner' because he got to keep the money in our business. After all, he wasn't sure it was the right thing to do from the start. But I didn't. I knew I was actually a 'winner,' too, because God knew our future and wanted the best for me. God knew that it would be a strain on our business at that time to spend a significant amount of money on a house."

"Sounds like you have a very patient husband. Sarah will agree when I tell you that I have never been open-minded when I think something isn't right for us. Why do I need to say a prayer when I already know something is wrong? Why can't I just say 'no'?"

"When we solve problems through prayer together, we feel closer to the Lord and one another, and there isn't any resentment as a result. It's a wonderful unifying factor in a marriage. After that incident, I loved my husband all the more because he was open to my desires, and cared about doing what the Lord wanted for us. If he had been stubborn and refused to look at my side of the decision, I could have been bitter and it would have driven a wedge into our marriage. With the prayer method of solving problems, we move closer together rather than further apart. We move towards a celestial marriage on earth.

"Sometimes the 'no' answers we receive are to prevent us from unknown devastating consequences that otherwise might happen. On this same occasion of praying to know if we should buy a house and move into a certain ward, we later found out that it wasn't just our finances the Lord was protecting. A year later, when we did move into that very same ward, we learned that a young man had just been sent to prison for molesting young boys. One of the incidents had occurred in the restroom at church! By the description and age of the other victims, we knew that our son would have been a prime target for the pedophile. Our precious eight year old, Alexander, could have been one of his victims if we had moved into the ward just one year prior. I have always felt that the Lord protected us from financial ruin and our son from being sexually abused. My husband and I thank the Lord constantly for answering our prayers and being part of our partnership in marriage.

"It is amazing how important timing can be. After we did move, the thought went through my mind, 'You will be called to serve in the Young Women's Organization.' The following Sunday, I was extended a call from the bishop to be the Laurel class advisor. I was so excited. As I met with my group of five Laurels, one of the girls (I will call Carrie), seemed troubled. At the time, I knew very little about sexual abuse, but the thought went through my mind from the Holy Spirit that she had been a victim. I started having her over to my house twice a week, to give her personal attention. She would follow me around the house, telling me what was on her mind as I tended my baby, made dinner, and finished my chores in the house.

"After six months I had won her trust, and she disclosed to me that her father had sexually abused her as a small child. My husband and I were able to get her placed in another home. Soon, she lost weight she didn't need. The foster mother taught her how to dress to augment her best features, and her self-esteem seemed to skyrocket. For the first time in her life, she had two people who believed her, understood her, and in whom she could place her trust. This story is yet to end happily ever after. But one thing I know, is that I was meant to be there at that time, to help this young girl.

"What if my husband hadn't wanted to move, and only thought about himself and the impact a move would have on him? I would have missed an important part of my mission in life. Marriage is about mutual support and the desire to help our spouse accomplish his or her destiny. And whether that mission is to one person or to many, it is equally important in the eyes of God."

Sarah asked, "But it still feels like one partner loses when they both get different answers. Couldn't one partner manipulate this process so they get their own way all the time?"

"I suppose that could happen in a relationship. But if it does, that kind of couple will never obtain a celestial marriage. Seeking the Lord's way is just that. It's not manipulating the answers. It's about listening."

"Can you give us an example?" Jake asked desperately.

"One year, Conrad and I were thinking about buying a film processing company. This enterprise seemed like the perfect addition to our own video production company. Adding this piece would enable us to make our own feature films from start to finish without relying on anyone else. When we prayed about it, I felt depressed and Conrad felt good. We knew that meant a 'no' from the Lord. But, Conrad really wanted this, so he continued to study it. He was obsessed. He wanted to make an offer, so he came up with some new figures which looked better on paper. I still felt depressed. Conrad consulted our accountant who said that our proposed offer was too high and could cause us problems if it was accepted. So, Conrad reworked the numbers again, and came up with a lower offer that would provide us the proper security. We prayed about it, and both felt peaceful. Conrad formally made the offer, with both of us united.

"As it turned out, our offer was too low and someone else bought the business. Just about that time, our other business took a small downturn. If we had paid the price necessary to buy the business, it might have meant financial ruin for us. Because we consulted with the Lord, and He advised us through an answer to our prayers, we didn't lose in the deal. I suppose my husband could have manipulated the deal to get me to go along, but we both have learned that you only win when you listen to the Lord.

"One of my friends told me once, 'Well that system works for you, but I'm the only spiritual one in our marriage. There's no way we could receive answers together.' She wanted to have six children and her husband didn't. Two was enough for him. On an issue so important as children, couples must be in harmony and agreement. But, she claimed that she knew there were more spirits waiting to come into their family. Purposely, she would deceive her husband to get pregnant. She felt that 'the ends justified the means.' She was trapped by her own vanity and being self-righteous. But, she didn't realize that she betrayed her relationship with her husband. She wasn't learning how to create a oneness in their marriage. She was creating disharmony by being deceptive. Additionally, she denied herself and her husband the opportunity of receiving revelation together. By exercising faith in the Lord, she would have known that if it was truly meant to be, both of them would receive the 'yes' answer from the Lord. If she had only been willing to discuss, study it out, and pray about it together, great things could have happened in their marriage and they might still be married today.

"When couples start out with open communication, humility, and a willingness to seek answers together, a great unity of marriage occurs. Remember, when we are married in the temple for eternity, it is only the promise of such. It is up to us to make it happen, and to create unity that will carry us through eternity. Making decisions together spiritually brings us closer to perfection in marriage and true oneness in purpose."

"I'm beginning to get it. But I need more examples," Jake demanded.

"Let me tell you about Evelyn. Her daughter Brittany was having trouble in school. Evelyn was concerned and started solving the problem herself. She felt that her husband Philip was too busy with his dental practice and his calling as stake Young Men's president to investigate the problem, so she decided to tackle it herself.

"First she had Brittany tested and discovered that she was severely dyslexic. Evelyn telephoned around the city and found the Hamlin Robinson School, which specialized in teaching children with dyslexia. It sounded like the perfect school for Brittany. She felt a surge like an adrenaline rush and identified it as the Holy Ghost testifying to her that this was the right school for Brittany.

"When she told Philip, he was totally opposed to Evelyn commuting so far away from home to drive Brittany to school every day. On top of that, he didn't accept the fact that she was dyslexic. Evelyn realized that she had made a serious mistake in not counseling with Philip during her investigations. She felt it was imprudent to argue and insist that she was right, or to bear testimony to him that she knew from the Lord that this was where Brittany should go. So she just said, 'okay.'

"That night in her private prayers Evelyn asked the Lord to help her convince Philip that this was right for Brittany, if she had received an answer from him. That Saturday she had to travel out of town on family business. This meant that Philip had to baby-sit Brittany. Due to his busy schedule, this was a rare occasion. It had been a long time since he had spent such a large block of time alone with his daughter.

"It was meant to be. When Evelyn came home that night, Philip confided to his wife that Brittany couldn't read at all. He was surprised. The Spirit testified to him that her testing results were correct. She was dyslexic. He knew her education needed intervention and was open to studying and reviewing all of their options. Together, they prayed and asked the Lord to bless them with a good feeling if it was the right school for Brittany. Then they visited the Hamlin Robinson School. While they were at the school, they both had the same overwhelming spiritual feeling in their hearts that it was right. The Lord had answered their prayers together. They knew that they were doing what the Lord wanted for Brittany that year."

"Can a partner ever receive a revelation first, and then when their spouse hears it they just know it's right?" Sarah asked as if she were hopeful Jake would be this way.

"Of course. The husband or wife may immediately feel a witness from the Holy Spirit that the revelation their spouse received is of the Lord. In these cases unity is the result and support follows."

Sarah seemed embarrassed. "I guess that I've felt that I knew something was right before, but Jake dug in his heels and wouldn't listen to me."

"I admit that I've been wrong, Sarah," Jake apologized. "I'm sorry for the pain that I've caused you over the years. But I never knew about praying about decisions together, not like we're learning today."

Sarah melted with Jake's apology and leaned over to kiss him tenderly.

"You're getting results already!" I laughed.

Jake smiled and then looked puzzled. "Okay... I'll play the bad guy. I don't understand how it would work for one partner to get the answer, and then the other one recognizes it without studying it out? I mean, Evelyn had to start all over again, because philip needed time to figure it out himself."

"Sometimes that's how it happens. But not always. Here's another example.

"One day I was wallowing in self pity. I was recovering from a bout of pneumonia and lying in bed. I could get up and perform a few chores, but I fatigued easily and would get depressed because I still wasn't totally well. Our son Alexander was a two-and-a-half-year old toddler who needed my attention at frequent intervals. Consequently, getting enough healing sleep was difficult during the day. Whenever it rained, water would leak up from the cracks in the basement floors. Since we lived in Seattle where rain was the norm, it meant that a pattern of puddles frequently dotted the cold cement floor. Every time I'd get out of bed to go to the bathroom, my feet would get wet in the middle of the night.

"When we first married, I scrambled to can fruit and vegetables, buy canned tuna on sale, and buy our wheat, powdered milk, and honey for food storage. My husband was a convert of only one year, and was surprised by my zeal. He teased me, but supported my compulsion wholeheartedly, proud that I really lived all of the commandments of the Lord. Now I knew that I was inspired, but at the time I sometimes thought I was just an overachiever, insisting that we have a full two-year supply of food instead of just one.

"For two years we had worked very hard to establish our business while earning almost nothing. Twenty-four months later, we had literally eaten all of our food storage. Although Conrad had been pounding the pavement making sales calls, he just couldn't seem to get started. Corporations and industries weren't interested in buying $35,000 promotional films.

"Today, it's hard to believe that video was uncommon then. Super eight millimeter cameras were the household item seen at every family gathering. Movies made for business were filmed in the 16 millimeter format. A sales program that cost $35,000 and six months to produce in 1978 could be done for $12,000 in six weeks in the 80's. No wonder few companies were buying! Nevertheless, we had great hopes of building a business together. Remarkably, we didn't rely on any kind of welfare, neither government nor church. We lived off of our food storage. Conrad had had the foresight to buy a house divided into a triplex, so the rent from the upstairs apartment paid for our mortgage, heat, and lights. But now our food was gone, and we hadn't made one film sale.

"Once again, envision me sick in bed with pneumonia, coughing, and praying to the Lord. I was miserable in every way. I was thirty years old, living in a dark, wet basement with no money. I thought about the other boyfriends I could have married. I was generally bemoaning my outcast state to the Lord when the thought went through my head: 'Stop feeling sorry for yourself. Get up out of your bed, and get yourself a job.' I knew that was the Holy Ghost speaking to me in my mind. I obeyed immediately.

"I can still see myself walking to the phone placed on top of the second-hand, red antiqued dresser I had proudly refinished our first year of marriage in an effort to match, by color, all of the free, mismatched furniture we had scrounged. I was weak and I felt faint. I telephoned to see if my teaching credentials were still in order. They were. In fact, they didn't expire for one more year. Then I called my friend Paula and told her I thought I'd start teaching ballet again. She replied supportingly, 'Great. Come out here to the suburbs where the kids are. I can get you twenty students just from my neighborhood.' To this day, I'll always be grateful to Paula for her act of support.

"When Conrad returned to the basement, he saw me on the phone. I told him about the experience I had just had. He smiled lovingly and said, 'I know you were inspired.' We hugged and felt an intense unity surge through our beings.

"This experience illustrates the fact that sometimes an answer will come to one member of the marriage first, and then when the other one hears about it, they immediately receive the confirmation that it is from the Lord."

Sarah was crying. "That's what I want us to be like!"

"Are you all right, honey?" Jake offered tenderly.

"I'm sorry. I don't mean to cry. To tell the truth, I don't always understand the difference between my emotions and real revelations from the Lord."

"First of all, emotional answers come in a variety of ways. Let's just say that a couple, Jenny and Todd, are looking for a house to buy. They walk into a gorgeous house that is a hundred and fifty thousand dollars more than they had planned on spending. But, the house is straight out of Better Homes and Garden, and Jenny falls in love with it. Her heart starts racing, her breath shortens, and she gets butterflies in her stomach. She wants it badly. As they pass from room to room, she gets more and more excited, working herself up into a frenzy. As they walk out of the house, she says that she feels wonderful about the house. She knows it is meant to be theirs. She thinks her feeling must be from the Holy Ghost. However, she is new at discerning a prompting from the Holy Spirit."

Sarah began to laugh. "That is clearly a case of *wanting*, not inspiration!"

"No kidding. If Jenny and Todd followed the 'study it out method' and then prayed about it, the Lord would bless them to not make a mistake. Even if Jenny still couldn't hear the right answer, her husband's 'no' answer from the Lord would avoid the mistake. But, if Jenny was sincere about humbling herself, and being open to the Spirit, once again when praying with her husband, the Lord would work through her emotionalism and she would receive a strong enough witness from the Holy Spirit to know it wasn't right. Praying together, they wouldn't make the mistake of buying a house that was beyond their budget."

"That's a great example of why praying together about a decision is better than receiving an answer alone," Jake added.

"The example I just mentioned illustrates the difference between a good feeling from the emotions of wanting something and that of a prompting from Holy Ghost. The reversal can also be true. We can pray and feel badly about a decision, and this too can be a false signal."

Jake threw up his hands. "This is too complicated."

"Yes, it seems that way at first, but when you truly understand the workings of the Spirit, and you practice listening to the Spirit, you will understand.

"While I was serving a mission in France, I had the opportunity to teach an intelligent nineteen year old girl, I'll call Marie Claire. In the discussions Marie Claire was excited to learn that God still spoke to us today through a modern-day prophet on earth. Born and raised a Catholic, she had bombarded her parents and priest with questions about the inconsistencies in the doctrine of Catholicism. She couldn't understand why God, Jesus Christ, and the Holy Ghost were one mystical being, when Christ was clearly depicted as a man in the Bible. She asked her priest how Jesus could be God the Father when they both appeared side by side to Stephen the Apostle when he was being stoned to death. When she heard that a fourteen-year-old boy, Joseph Smith, had a vision in which he saw God the Father and Jesus Christ, His Son, her heart soared. For the first time in her life she felt no confusion. Every discussion filled her with the same overwhelming clarity and joy. However, as she approached baptism, and prayed to know if the church was true, her parents threw a fit. They told her that if she joined the Church of Jesus Christ of Latter-Day Saints, she would be doomed to hell. Marie Claire felt tremendous anxiety. She had knots in her stomach. She told us that when she prayed, all she could feel was sick inside. Did that mean that the Lord was telling her not to join the church? Or, was this an emotional answer coming from within herself?

"I know that it was an emotional answer, but I can't explain why," Sarah offered.

"Remember that I told you that she was born and raised a Catholic? In France, being a Catholic is part of their identity and has been so for hundreds of years. They are steeped in the tradition of being born a Catholic and dying a Catholic. When she told her parents that she was changing her religion, she felt for the first time the implications of her decision. Marie Claire's stomach churned inside as she worried about family rejection. For a time these emotions were so intense she could not recall the many witnesses she had felt from the Holy Ghost during the discussions testifying to her that the Church was true and that it was right for her to be baptized. After I taught her how to discern anxiety from revelation, she was able to identify the knots in her stomach as negative emotions and fear of an unknown future. Relieved by this revelation she once again felt the supreme feelings of joy from the Holy Ghost that she had experienced in studying the Gospel.

Jake heaved a heavy sigh. "I need more examples."

"As technology has changed, my husband and I have been constantly faced with the challenge of upgrading our equipment in our video production business. In 1998, we decided to buy a High Definition editing suite, one of the first in the United States and an investment of a million and a half dollars. We prayed and asked God if this decision was right. We had to be sure. The Lord answered our prayers with a peaceful feeling. However, a few days later when my husband took on the responsibility of making it all happen, he was filled with knots in his stomach due to this immense risk. This can happen when we forge ahead to new uncomfortable experiences. And, it is this anticipation, not the decision itself, that can cause anxiety. Remember, when a decision is right, it does not necessarily erase the difficulty that comes later in accomplishing the task."

Sarah interrupted. "I get it. Like breaking up with a boyfriend. You know it's right but you feel knots in your stomach because it's hard to do."

"But what if you get the anxiety feeling first? You know, before you have a good feeling from the Holy Ghost?" Jake was testing me.

"In order to receive revelation we must be open vessels willing to place our faith in the Lord 100%. Some people doubt their own abilities to receive revelation. This blocks their ability to hear the answer and heightens their anxiety level which is caused by self-doubt, not revelation."

"I have a friend like that," Sarah interjected. "Janet, my best friend in high school, grew up in an idyllic LDS family. You know, she was the kind of girl who grew up just knowing the Church was true. She never really had to pray to get answers for anything because she just followed the commandments, you know what I mean, the basic Mormon plan to happiness. Then one day her husband had a job offer from a start up company. It meant more money and incredible growth potential. They prayed about it, but Janet was so scared and nervous, all she could think about was the risk of working for a new company. She closed her mind telling her husband that she felt too sick to hear any answer. They played it safe and didn't make the move. The company was Microsoft. To this day, Janet's husband still begrudgingly reminds his wife that they could have been numbered among the Microsoft millionaires of today."

"Perfect example, Sarah. There are many couples who fall into this category. They live a safe predictable life, hide their talents, and never fulfill the measure of their creation because they are too scared or anxious to trust in their ability to receive an answer from the Lord. If, on the other hand, that couple had prayed sincerely and open-mindedly, and then received a 'no' answer, there would be no regrets.

"Now I want to tell you an example that is sacred to me. It's a story of how we can overcome emotionalism to feel the Spirit of the Holy Ghost. Conrad and I decided to marry in the Swiss temple. The Seattle Temple didn't exist at the time and we had no ties to any other temple.

Since my parents had taken me to the Swiss Temple right after my mission, it had become my dream to marry there. Conrad and I were so excited about the romantic adventure ahead of us. My whole life, I had envisioned my glorious wedding day in the temple. And now we were finally there.

"As we arrived at the temple, the President insisted that we had it wrong. Our wedding would have to be that night, rather than at the 10:00 a.m. appointment we had scheduled through the mail. Confused and very disappointed, my mother and father managed to lift our spirits by taking us motor touring through the beautiful countryside.

"That evening we were once again excited and happy. After going through an endowment session together, we hugged each other in the Celestial Room. Finally we were led to a sealing room where we would be married for time and all eternity. It was going to be so spiritual and special, just Conrad and me, and my parents at our wedding. Instead, we entered the room to see two other couples waiting in the room to be sealed. They were service men and their wives who had been married for a number of years. They had children and were temporarily stationed in Germany. They were finally being sealed together for eternity. I was so surprised to see other couples in my room at my wedding. Instantly I felt as if we were all just lumped together for an assembly line wedding. It wasn't what I had anticipated at all. In fact, I was in such shock I motioned to Conrad to follow me. We returned to the Celestial Room and my parents, sensitive to my feelings, came out to support me without me even saying anything.

"I started to cry, I was so disappointed. My wedding day wasn't going to be intimate and special. Suddenly, I felt like a number. My heart was heavy and my emotions were so strong. If I hadn't known better, I could have misinterpreted these events and feelings as a witness from the Lord that I shouldn't marry Conrad. What saved me in those moments of unhappiness? I had had a strong swelling in my heart, that 'whoosh' feeling that I know is a 'yes' from the Holy Spirit, when I had prayed about whether or not to marry Conrad.

"As Conrad was consoling me, the Temple President burst into our circle and brusquely and impatiently said, 'Well, do you want to be married or not?' He looked at us sternly, bereft of any compassion or understanding. We acquiesced, following him into the sealing room. I cried during the other sealings. Finally, the Temple President called our names. His countenance lacked emotion. He seemed to be in a hurry to just get us over with. I remember the sheer disappointment I was feeling. It felt as if this was the Las Vegas version of the sacred temple ceremony.

By this time my face was blotchy red from all my crying. I tried to choke back my tears. I was no longer a blushing bride, just a number in the Temple.

"And then it happened. As we were kneeling at the altar and the Temple President was pronouncing the words that bound us together forever, the most powerful witness I have ever felt from the Holy Ghost filled my soul with such intensity that it penetrated through all of my emotional disappointments and tears. I knew at that moment that the Lord wanted me to absolutely know that I was doing what he wanted me to do. And so, for a few moments, I was wrapped in a cocoon of Heavenly Father's love and transported into a celestial realm. I felt that I was being married into a partnership with my husband and the Lord. God was there for me at the most important occasion of my life. His tender mercy is so powerful that He made sure that His witness of the Holy Spirit penetrated my emotions so that I would know that I had made the right choice.

"In spite of what seemed to be party crashers at my wedding and the insensitivity of a Temple President, I had a few moments when it was just my husband, the Lord, and me. And that incredible gift of the Spirit during those few moments overcame all of the human foibles and follies of the day. When I look back, I can easily forgive the humanness of the Temple President, who was probably tired, overworked, and yet still gave service the best way he knew how. That day the Lord took care of me through the Spirit of the Holy Ghost. God made up for the apparent disaster and insensitivity of man."

I paused and the room filled with silence. Jake was looking down at the Bokhara Persian carpet beneath his Nike-clad feet. Had I shared a story too personal, too sacred? Did they understand? I was beginning to feel like a seamstress who had just finished a designer suit, when her two-year-old decides to practice his cutting skills on the skirt. Jake glanced up. His soulful eyes penetrated my being with great intensity.

"You are so close to the Spirit. You know the difference between emotionalism and true promptings from God. You make it sound easy."

"If it were that easy, I wouldn't have waited until two weeks before a wedding to understand the promptings of the Spirit! Don't be discouraged. It will come to you too. You and your wife will learn to receive revelation together and it will be a great unifying factor in your marriage."

"What happened after your wedding? Were you still disappointed it didn't turn out the way you had dreamed it would be?" Sarah wanted to know.

"Conrad and I took a five week honeymoon, touring France, Italy, and Greece. It was meant to be. During that time, we experienced events that empowered us with spiritual insights, insights that would establish a firm foundation for a celestial marriage on earth.

"Like many brides, I practically thought that birds would be singing at our wedding and angels surely would be in the room with us. I imagined us soaring to a new level of spirituality, even close to making our calling and election sure. How naive I was. Little did I know that this experience was to become another valued lesson.

"When we arrived in Italy on our honeymoon, we were in awe of the great works of art created by Michaelangelo, Raphael, Leonardo Da Vinci, and others. We marveled at the paintings on the Sistine Chapel ceiling. We stood on the Roman Forum floors and witnessed the remains of a once great Roman Empire. We were bowled over by the splendor of the architecture, both Roman and Florentine. The greatness of those eras was bountiful. Yet, in contrast, the Italy of today was a model of decline, lacking anything comparable in beauty, art, or success.

"It made us think about the scripture, '*Lay up for yourself treasures in heaven where moth and dust do not corrupt.*' A mighty civilization was gone. Only hollow ruins remained to tell the story of a once great country. We thought of the many people who ended up like the Roman ruins, nothing more than hollow, empty shells crumbling on the outside. Sadly, some of the once famous movie stars, politicians, architects, and authors, ended up, when their day in the sun was over, in a pile of ruins. We thought about the truly great people. They were the ones who learned to love, forgive, and serve others, the true building blocks of a rich life.

"We searched for the modern geniuses of art and architecture in Italy where visitors came to see the past. We reveled in the beauty of the Renaissance and the masterpieces created by them, but we couldn't find much of what modern Italians had achieved since the Renaissance. It was as if the Lord was telling us that we could never rest on our past achievements. It was as if God was inspiring us to never stop growing, learning and perfecting our gifts. It was then that we realized our wedding was just the beginning, not the end goal. We knew that we did not want to have a marriage that, in 50 years, would be like a pile of ancient stone rubble, a hollow Parthenon. We vowed to each other that we would do everything we could to develop our gifts and talents and support each other. We would never achieve success and then stop, only to experience decline and decay like the Roman Empire."

"Do you learn from everything you do?"

"Not always," I laughed. "But I sure try to.

"During the last eight years I have taught the Family Relations Class in our ward with an emphasis on celestial marriage. Many couples have been through my class. There is a sharp contrast between the ones who catch the vision and learn how to solve their problems together using prayer and the ones who don't.

"During my second year of teaching, two couples entered my class at the bishop's request. Couple number one I shall call Carla and Paul. When I began to teach the lesson on solving problems, they volunteered that they were having trouble in their marriage and were practically not speaking to each other. Carla wanted another child and Paul did not. They didn't know how to solve their problem.

"As a class, we wrote on the chalkboard the pros and cons. On the pro side, Carla said: 1. She wanted to have all of her children early and get it over with so that she could still be young when the children were teenagers. Then, she could pursue her own dreams. 2. She was afraid she would not be able to have any more children unless she hurried and had them now.

"Paul eagerly volunteered the cons: 1. They were financially deep in debt. He felt strongly that they couldn't afford another child right now. He wanted to get out of debt first. 2. He felt that his wife was not emotionally ready to handle another baby when they already had two under the age of three. 3. Carla had suffered with poor health during both pregnancies. He wanted her to have time to recover physically and mentally. 4. He wanted more time to adjust to marriage and the two babies they already had.

"I asked them to go home and figure out which was the right answer for them at this time in their lives, and then pray and ask if it was right. I emphasized in the class that there would be no winner or loser. The Lord wanted them to be happy together and to lead to a successful life. The next week, we were all anxious to hear about their spiritual experience. Instead, to our disappointment, they had failed to even try."

"Why?"

"Paul decided that it wasn't right to ask his wife to choose his solution to the problem, and yet he didn't feel right about her choice. Carla, on the other hand, was willing to pray and ask if it was right for them to wait until they were out of debt and she had recovered fully from having the other two children. In spite of her willingness, Paul wouldn't budge. His close-mindedness kept them from even trying to receive revelation from the Lord.

"Unfortunately, this stymied their progress in learning how to receive revelation to better govern their lives and make wise decisions according to what the Lord knew was best for them and their future.

"What happened to them?"

"Last I heard, they moved to California and Paul gave in to his wife's wishes. The couple had another baby. Their finances were worse than ever, and she was still on an emotional roller coaster and physically ill frequently. All of this unhappiness could have been avoided if they had just used the prayer method to solve their problems. One can almost predict that the strain on their marital partnership will increase over the years, and may end in divorce unless they learn how to make major decisions as a team, using the help of the Lord.

"Another couple I'll call Freddie and Gina came to my class with another classic problem. Freddie was finishing up his medical internship at Swedish Hospital. He had decided to take a job offer in Idaho without consulting his wife Gina. He figured that it was his decision. Gina was extremely upset. It meant leaving her parents in Seattle and spending the rest of her life in what she considered to be a backwoods state. Gina was a college graduate, had a model's figure, and always looked as if she had just stepped out of *Vogue* magazine. Freddie was a returned missionary, had a fine intellect, but couldn't see why they had to pray about this decision together. He felt that he had already received a confirmation from the Spirit that they were to move to Idaho. So what was the point? As the class progressed, Freddie stopped coming. He didn't want to face a class that had challenged him to study out the pros and cons of moving to Idaho and accepting this job offer. He simply refused to pray about it with his wife. Freddie claimed to have experienced a witness by the Holy Spirit to move, but his wife had not. She resented his controlling authoritarian behavior bitterly. Freddie owed Gina a chance to go through the prayer process as a team."

"I can see now that he shouldn't have had any fear praying as a team, knowing the Lord wanted both of them to be winners and happy with the decision," Jake commented.

"You're really understanding this process now, Jake."

"I think that Gina was also at fault," Sarah added.

"How so?" I asked to see if Sarah understood.

"She was so closed-minded about the possibility of living in Idaho that she also couldn't receive an answer from the Spirit."

"You are so right, Sarah. In fact, in every class she continued to complain about how her husband had wronged her. They finally did move to Idaho where he's practicing medicine. They too are a time bomb of inability to solve problems together that will blow up in their faces years from now unless they make critical changes.

"These two couples are common examples of temple marriages moving on a secular pathway to disharmony, rather than moving on the pathway of celestial perfection together.

"So far, I have only discussed the most common way of receiving answers to our prayers, and that is through the Gift of the Holy Ghost prompting us."

"Are there other ways that our prayers can be answered together?" Sarah quizzed me intently.

"Yes, there are other very important ways that the Lord answers our prayers. In fact, the most common way our prayers are answered, when we are young, is that we are simply granted our request, from the Lord. For example, a girl might pray that she will remember all of the material she has been studying in History class so that she can do well on the test. She takes the test and receives an 'A.' Children usually aren't making major decisions in their lives, but they have needs. The Lord knows that they are neophytes in understanding the workings of the Spirit, so He has tender mercy on them. Sometimes they just need to be comforted so they can go to sleep. Sometimes they need help with a bully at school, to get a part in the school play, win a science contest, or help a friend with problems. The list is endless."

"Are you saying that our prayers won't be answered in that way because we are no longer children?" Sarah asked.

"No, of course not. Sometimes our problems are not about studying out a problem and determining the best solution. Sometimes they are about expediency. One of my girlfriends was five months pregnant and having severe trouble with kidney stones. She landed in the hospital, doubled over in pain. She called me on the phone and said that she didn't know what she was going to do. She hadn't been able to pass the kidney stone, so the doctor was either going to have to administer radiation or perform surgery. In the first scenario, the radiation could harm the baby. In the second, the operation could mean that she'd have to stay in bed for the rest of her pregnancy. I told my girlfriend that neither option was acceptable. The radiation was too dangerous to the baby, and she couldn't afford to stay in bed when she already had four children at home who needed attention. I told her that I knew the Lord would help her pass the kidney stone that night and promised her that I would pray for this to happen. She wondered how I could be so sure. I quizzed her about her adherence to the commandments, cementing what I already knew. She was a righteous woman. Then I quoted her Section 82, verse 10 of the *Doctrine and Covenants.* 'I, the Lord, am bound when ye do what I say.' Then I told her that since she was a partner in bringing this spirit into the world with the Lord, and He knew that the other options weren't realistic, He would create the miracle and she would pass the stones that night. I got off the phone and knelt down on my kitchen floor and asked the Lord to grant this request. The next day she called and said that she passed the stones just before midnight.

"Sometimes what we ask for is not granted by the Lord and then we know it is a 'no' answer. George and Matty wanted to buy a certain house. They put down some earnest money on the house and then prayed to know if they had made the right decision. The next day the real estate agent called and said that the deal had fallen through. This is a heavenly way of having our prayers answered.

"The third, most common way of receiving answers to our prayers, is through our spouse, a friend, a Bishop, mother, or father, or a person who seems to float into our life for just a brief time, long enough to tell us the answer the Lord wants us to hear. When we hear the advice, we receive a witness from the Holy Spirit testifying to us that the advice is from the Lord and the answer to our problem.

"One day I came home from teaching ballet and went to bed early because I had a severe headache. Two hours later I awoke suddenly. I felt compelled to get up, go to the telephone, and call Sister Titera, a lady in our ward. I barely knew her, having only heard her give outstanding Relief Society lessons. Two weeks earlier, my mother had called to see if there was a single, older woman in our ward who would be a good match for the Patriarch of her Stake, a widower who was a very lonely man. I didn't know of anyone at the time. Now I found myself on the phone telling Sister Titera all about Gus Carlston, the 70 year old Patriarch. She said that she had just been on her knees praying to the Lord, asking him to provide a husband for her. I invited her to dinner at my parents' house to meet him. The rest is history. They fell in love and were married in the temple."

"I guess you're an answer to our prayer too," Sarah interjected.

"How so?"

"Well, two weeks ago, after our last fight, I had been crying all morning. Intermittently, I was praying and asking Father in Heaven to help us. That's when you came to the door."

"That's very kind of you. I do know that you are very special people and you can make your marriage a joyful union. You are already learning to become one in spirit."

"Are there other ways our prayers are answered?" Jake asked.

"The fourth way that is common to receive answers to our prayers is authored by the Holy Spirit, and comes to us in the form of a thought that flows through our mind."

"Like what?" Jake continued asking.

"Another story. Ready? After waiting for two years, the church adoption agency called to announce that they had a baby girl for us. We wanted to know that this little girl was indeed the child the Lord wanted us to adopt into our family. So, we asked for time to pray about it. First, we prayed together as a family. All of us received an indescribable feeling of happiness that filled our whole being. We knew we were supposed to adopt this little girl. But I think that the Lord knew I needed something more. That night at approximately 3:00 AM, I seemed to be awakened. I sat straight up in bed, and this thought went through my head: 'This little girl was foreordained to be in your family. She will love you in the same way that you love your own mother. She will be talented, and she will always be grateful that you adopted her into your family.' Then it ended. I woke Conrad up and rehearsed the revelation to him. He cried tears of joy, and so did I. Then, both of us were filled with a 'whoosh' from the Holy Spirit, testifying to us that this revelation was from the Lord!"

"I don't mean to always play the devil's advocate, but how do you know that you didn't just make that up in your mind yourself? You know, with your own mind, as in just thinking?"

"That is a very good question, and this is the answer: when the thought comes from the Lord, it flows through my mind steadily and without interruption and feels like the Lord is giving me a priesthood blessing directly. When one is just thinking one's own thoughts, the thoughts are sporadic, and often disjointed. Secondly, I never forget the words in a revelation. I can repeat them exactly as they were delivered in my mind forever. Thirdly, there is always an accompanying sign from the Holy Spirit, testifying to me that what flowed through my mind was from the Holy Spirit and not me. It is that 'whoosh' feeling I have come to identify as being from the Lord. This is how it works in me. You will have to discover how it works in you."

"Thanks for those guidelines. What else?" Jake looked intent on learning more.

"A fifth way of receiving answers to our prayers is through reading the scriptures. Recently, Conrad and I had the opportunity to meet someone prominent who could advance our careers. Before we left for the meeting, we asked a friend to give Conrad a blessing. In the blessing from the Lord, Conrad was promised that he and this person would develop a project together. But, at the meeting, it didn't happen. As the months ticked by, we were both feeling discouraged and began to think that we had misheard the blessing from the Lord. Six months later as we were reading the scriptures during our couple's daily scripture reading, we re-read the story about how Nephi had to return to Jerusalem to obtain the plates of brass. On the first attempts, Nephi and his brothers totally failed. Wow! Did they fail, big time. They lost all of the family's gold and jewels when they were supposed to trade them for the brass plates, the genealogy of their family, and the scriptures of all of the prophets since the beginning of time.

"Outside the city his brothers regarded him as a total failure. And no way, no how, were they going to have anything to do with getting the plates again. But, not Nephi! What a man, what a self-assured faithful man. He was ready to go back, in spite of the first failure. He was willing to try again because he knew that God commanded him to do so. So, he knew that the Lord would provide a way. And of course, as we know, Nephi succeeded.

"When Conrad and I read that story, we looked at each other and said almost simultaneously, 'We don't need to worry. The Lord gave the blessing. It will happen in due time.' And immediately, a peace came over both of us testifying from the Holy Ghost that it was right.

"A Patriarchal Blessing is another great way to receive answers to prayers. A beautiful young lady, I'll call Jill, who had returned from her mission in Belgium, was feeling blue and wondering if she really was supposed to have gone on a mission for the Lord. After all, she had not converted one single person on her mission. Jill's mother called me and asked me to talk to her. She knew that I had had a very hard mission in France and thought that I could cheer her up. I asked Jill to bring her Patriarchal Blessing with her.

"We started with a prayer and had a wonderful time sharing stories and experiences that were similar. Then, I told her that I felt that she was meant to go on a mission, not just to the people in Belgium, but to learn how to teach the gospel so that she could teach someone at home. I told her that after my mission, I had met a young man who was spiritually searching for answers. I taught him the gospel and he joined the church. Later, he became my husband. I knew then that I was meant to go on a mission so that I would know how to teach him.

"We read Jill's Patriarchal Blessing to see if the Lord had something to say about it. After reading just a few sentences, I just about fell over. There it was, the answer, in black and white. It said that she would go out into the world as a missionary in order that she might return and be able to teach the gospel to many of her friends and neighbors. We both cried in the glory of the Lord's ways. She is a beautiful young woman who has many wonderful, as yet unwritten, stories of conversions ahead of her.

"Priesthood blessings are another source of answers and a necessity in our household. I can't imagine a month without someone in our family needing help from the Lord and asking for a blessing. We have come to rely on the direct revelation the Lord can give to us in a blessing. In my early thirties, my friend Janet, who had moved to Arizona, began to confide in me over the phone. She thought her husband was having an affair on his out of town business trips. One day she asked me to go over to a mutual friend's house, and ask if this friend's daughter was the one having an affair with Janet's husband. Being terribly naive at the time, I obeyed Janet's request. The friend confirmed the dreadful news. I can still see myself dialing Janet's telephone number in Arizona. She didn't seem at all surprised. The next thing I knew, she had packed up the furniture and five children, and moved back to Seattle. She only left a note in the empty house saying: 'You know what you did.' Divorce papers were immediately filed.

"I felt sick about it. I felt as if it was my fault because I had been the bearer of bad tidings. It was so traumatic for me, that I literally started to have severe heart pains. I felt as if my heart was breaking, and I knew what the great authors of literature meant when they described a heroine dying of a broken heart. The pains increased until I was rendered immobile. Conrad rushed me to emergency. I was diagnosed with endocarditis. This whole incident was utterly devastating to me mentally and physically. Conrad and I had our little boy, but hadn't been able to have any more children. We had begun a long process of fertility treatments so that I could get pregnant again. Now, with this new health problem, I had to terminate the treatments and be treated for the heart condition.

"When we returned home, I felt taken care of physically, but not mentally. I needed the Lord's help. Conrad immediately gave me a blessing from the Lord. It was direct revelation telling me what I had to do. I was told to remove myself from the situation. It was not in my power to help them and I needed to take care of my own health so that I could finish my mission on earth. As the blessing ended, I felt a great peace come over me, and I was able to let go of their problem.

"How grateful I was to have the power of the Priesthood in my home. How grateful I was to have a righteous husband who was willing to help me solve my problems anytime and anyplace."

"I think I see why we have to understand every way our prayers are answered," Sarah volunteered.

"Me too," Jake chimed in. "We have to know and understand every way because different circumstances need answers in different ways. Duh... I guess that sounds obvious."

"Don't be so hard on yourself. We wouldn't be having this conversation if it was easy. The fact is that we all have to learn how to receive revelation individually, and as a couple. I saved the least common ways of receiving answers to prayers for last.

"Sometimes the Lord answers our prayers through a dream. This is a medium which must be accompanied by the Holy Spirit to testify that it is, indeed, of the Spirit. I have counseled people who think they have had a dream from the Lord. But, on further investigation, they have discovered that the dream had no purpose, or was convoluted or weird, and they didn't have any kind of Holy Ghost feeling, witnessing to them that it was of the Lord.

"A week before my mother died of cancer I had a dream in which I saw myself sitting by my mother's bed in a hospice care center. Suddenly, the spirit of my father appeared at the foot of her bed. He smiled and said, 'Laura, the Lord your God loves you.' Then my mother's spirit appeared by his side and she looked so healthy and happy. She was no longer in her cancerous, emaciated body. I looked at the bed and could see that she had died. Then, I looked back at my parents and saw them turn and walk down a long corridor that led to infinity. After the dream ended, I woke up and sat up in bed. A 'whoosh' feeling from the Holy Spirit came over me, testifying that this was a dream from the Lord and would come to pass. The dream's purpose was to comfort me. It was simple and direct, and I received a confirmation from the Holy Spirit.

"In 1999, Conrad and I felt we should expand our business in Los Angeles by buying a building for a post production facility. For almost two years, Conrad had been commuting to LA three days a week to work on his television series, *National Desk*. We prayed about our decision and felt a confirmation from the Spirit. After looking for six months for the right building, we were feeling discouraged and questioned our initial revelation. All our offers to purchase properties were unsuccessful.

"We called a different real estate agent, and asked him if he knew of any properties that hadn't been listed yet. He knew of one coming on the market in a week that sounded perfect. We flew down to LA to check it out. Once again, we made an offer. We told the real estate agent how much we wanted to offer plus five reasons why it would be beneficial for the owner to accept our deal. The agent agreed to present the offer on Thursday and ask for the owner's answer on Friday. Thursday night I had a dream in which I saw our real estate agent presenting our offer. But, instead of representing us, and our five reasons to accept the deal, he told the owner to counter with a higher amount. I woke up shocked that the agent had misrepresented us. I recounted the dream to Conrad. Sure enough, at the office that day, we received a call from the agent asking for $100,000 more to close the deal. Of course, we said 'no.' Because the Lord allowed me to see the future in a dream, it showed us that we were on the right track, and that the Lord was indeed with us in our pursuit. Furthermore, it was clear in the dream that this was not the right building or agent for us. It was a second witness that our initial revelation to expand our business was from the Lord. Two months later, a remarkable new piece of property came on the market on my birthday. We were the first to look at it, and instantly knew that the Lord had provided it for us. It was twice the size of the other buildings and a fraction of the cost per square foot. We truly knew that the Lord had blessed us.

"Every time I have ever had a dream from the Lord, it had a purpose. Subsequently, I have awakened, and a strong witness from the Holy Spirit has testified to me that it was true. We have to be very careful not to jump to conclusions that just any dream is from the Lord. Our subconscious minds are so powerful that we can have very colorful and interesting dreams. But that is all they are most of the time, just interesting dreams.

"Sometimes one will receive a revelation from the Lord in the form of a vision in the mind. This is not a vision like Joseph Smith had in which he literally saw God the Father, and his Son, Jesus Christ in person. This is like having a dream while you are wide-awake. You only see it inside your mind. If anyone else was in the room, they wouldn't have a clue what you were experiencing in the private recesses of your mind. One summer, I became very ill with pneumonia, and ran a very high temperature for three days. Conrad and our daughter Elisabeth drove me to the doctor's office, helped me into a patient room and then left to accomplish errands. While I was all alone waiting for my X-rays to be ready for the doctor's viewing, I suddenly saw my deceased mother in my mind. She was standing by my side. I was astonished at how beautiful she was. I began to speak to her in my mind. As if it were mental telepathy, I said, 'Oh mother! You're so beautiful.' She responded, 'It's like that here.' I continued, 'Mom, I'm so sorry that I wasn't a good nurse for you when you were dying. I'm not like you in that way.' (My mother had been a very gifted registered nurse.) She smiled warmly, 'Oh no, you were wonderful, and I will always be grateful for the sacrifice you made in taking care of me.' I asked if Dad was there. She said that he was, and motioned to the corner of the room. He had one foot in the patient room and one foot in the corridor that led to infinity. He looked so busy! He had that look I had seen many times when he was a Bishop, weighed down with people's problems. The first words out of his mouth were, 'Laura, we can only stay a minute.' I replied, 'Oh Dad. Please take me with you.' (At that point I just wanted to die.) I continued, 'It would be so easy to be on the other side, being like a guardian angel, just going around helping people.' His next words pierced my soul and changed my life forever. 'It isn't what you think it is here. You can be far more effective in helping people to change their lives on earth than you can here.' Then, I asked him if he still loved me and he assured me that he and mother loved me more than I would ever know. Next, my attention was diverted back to my mother. She smiled and said, 'You're going to be okay.' Then my mind went blank for a few seconds. As the doctor walked into the room, a powerful feeling from the Holy Spirit came over me, testifying that I had had a true vision in my mind.

"Later, when I told Conrad this experience. He, too, felt a warm feeling come over him, testifying that the vision in my mind was from the Lord. We hugged and felt a special closeness to the Spirit.

"The least common way to receive answers to prayers is by an actual vision, such as Joseph Smith experienced, in which a messenger from the Lord delivers a message personally. Some people have actually heard an audible voice. A good example of this is in the scriptures. Samuel heard the voice of the Lord three times until he stopped confusing it for Eli's voice and called out to the Lord, 'speak; for thy servant heareth.'" (I Samuel 3:10).

"You know I love those stories," said Sarah ever so sweetly, "But I'm more grateful to learn for ourselves how to listen to the Holy Spirit and receive answers as a couple."

"That's very perceptive of you Sarah, because probably ninety-nine percent of the time our prayers are answered with the inspiration of the Holy Spirit. As a couple working towards perfection, striving for oneness, and desiring to follow the Lord's will, praying to solve your problems together will bring the following benefits: unity, closeness with the Lord and each other; and an assurance that your decisions are correct, thereby avoiding serious mistakes. I know from personal experience that the Lord always answers our prayers, wants us to be successful, and is indeed our third partner in our celestial marriages on earth. I know that using prayer together to solve our problems is the tool the Lord has given us to increase our love for each other and achieve a constant harmony and oneness in marriage.

The ornate grandfather's clock began to chime. Excusing myself, I left Sarah and Jake with their third assignment.

ASSIGNMENT NUMBER THREE:

Pray about all decisions as a couple. Remember that there is never a winner and a loser. You are both winners, no matter what the answer is from the Lord, because He knows the future and He wants the best for both of you.

Follow these steps:

1. Be open-minded to the ideas and desires of your spouse.

2. Study out the options for both sides of an issue.

3. Make a decision together, based on research, wisdom, and what seems to be best for both of you.

4. Pray about the decision, asking the Lord if it is right in your nightly couple's prayer.

5. Monitor your feelings from the Spirit and share them with each other.

6. If you both feel a peaceful feeling, a good feeling, a euphoric feeling, a swelling feeling in the heart, a "just knowing it's right" feeling etc., then you have made the right decision.

7. If one or both of you feels irritable about the decision, agitated, depressed, unhappy, miserable, cries about the decision, or even just plain forgets about it as if it doesn't matter anymore, then the decision is wrong and you must try again as a couple to make another decision. The Lord works in unity with a couple.

~

CHAPTER 4

GOAL SETTING

"Today I will be talking about the fourth secret to obtaining a successful celestial marriage: goal setting."

Jake covered his ears as if the sounds I had uttered were painful. He laid down his pen and pronounced adamantly, "I thought you were inspired until now. Excuse me while I take a nap."

Laughing, I continued. "When someone verbalizes the word, 'Goals,' many people's eyes begin to roll and glaze over. It brings out the worst in some of us. We dig our heels into the ground, grit our teeth, and yell out, 'Not now. I'm too busy.' Most people just don't want to be pressed into writing down their aspirations, dreams and desires. This is normal. Not just because we want to rebel or because we're lazy, but because deep inside, none of us want to fail. That is the bottom line! We fear the failure of not reaching a goal. We fear the shame we might face from our peers, especially if they see us set a goal to do something and then we fail. It's like saying we're going to lose ten pounds, and instead we gain fifteen!"

"What? You knew?" Sarah demanded.

"Knew what?" I asked.

"That I gained fifteen pounds after losing ten," Sarah blurted out. I just shook my head.

"You see. That's why I never set goals. Then I can't fail," Jake proudly announced.

"Sounds reasonable! Don't set goals and you'll have high self-esteem. But, nothing could be further from the truth. We all know the feelings of satisfaction when we achieve even the smallest accomplishment. When a baby learns to walk, he is so proud of himself. The baby smiles and coos in baby gibberish. Although the baby didn't write down the goal, 'I will be able to walk at ten months,' he actually did formulate a goal and tried until he accomplished it. Completed goals build our self-esteem and give us impetus to strive for loftier heights. So, if they make us feel good, why do we avoid making them as if they were a nasty case of influenza?

"I believe that even more than fear, we avoid goal setting sessions because it is so hard to stay on course, without support. Think about how much support a baby gets when he or she begins to walk. We go out of our way to cheer them on. But later in life, we lose that natural support system given to us by our parents. That's why we need a partner to help us. We need a partner who knows us inside and out, who is our constant support, whose mission in life includes seeing that we accomplish our mission. We need goals that are set with our eternal mate. It makes all the difference in the world."

Jake was testy. "Make goals with your mate? Are you crazy? They will harass you and hound you until you're so miserable that you'd wish you'd never set the goal. I told Sarah I'd clean out the garage once, and I never heard the end of it."

"Did you get it done?"

"Well, yeah."

"I rest my case." I continued: "Remember when you were first married, you would talk about what you were going to do in life, how you were going to raise the children, how you were going to support each other in school before the children came? In fact, even before that, by the very act of getting married, together you planned and accomplished one of your most important goals in life: marrying in the temple for eternity."

Jake began to listen to me begrudgingly.

"It's natural, from those beginnings, to continue the process by starting the habit of a yearly planning session with your spouse. Some researchers have found that only three percent of Americans write down goals on paper and less than one percent review their goals each day.[2] Have you ever noticed that it is a similar percentage of people in the USA who are highly successful? Goals, written down, with the strength of faith, and the conviction of two mission-oriented people, is an unsinkable combination."

Sarah interrupted. "Do you and your husband set goals together?"

"My husband and I started goal setting as a couple our first year of marriage. Each year we spend a day reviewing the past, and setting goals

[2] Brian Tracy, "A Strategy for Goal Achievement " (*Nightingale-Conant's Insight* #94) pg. 11

for the new year. We also set five-year goals, ten-year goals and even twenty-year goals. As soon as the children came, we spent one day as part of an annual honeymoon during which we would review the year's progress and assess what we had accomplished, and what we now needed to work on. At first, we couldn't afford anything fancy. My mother would take our little baby, and we would take one day off to go camping. Now we have progressed to more exotic vacations and settings for our goal planning sessions. One of our best was sitting on a white stucco terrace on the island of Santorini in Greece. The setting was inspiring and served as a catalyst to create new goals."

"Well, vacations like that could make goal setting almost palatable," Jake laughed heartily.

I was hoping that I had hooked him and continued. "When you set goals, they should focus on what your partnership wants to accomplish together, as well as what you want individually. It is pointless for a husband to have a goal to lose ten pounds by the end of the year, if his wife doesn't have a goal to help him by cooking low-fat meals. Teamwork is the name of the game in goal planning. After planning goals as a married couple and having the incredible support of my husband, I wouldn't want to have to do it alone again!"

"Is there a precedent for goal-setting in the scriptures?" Sarah asked.

"Absolutely. It starts in the pre-mortal world when Father in Heaven had a goal planning session with us. In the *Pearl of Great Price*, Moses 1:39 'For behold, this is my work and my glory – to bring to pass the immortality and eternal life of man,' it clearly defines God's number one goal. Then we read about a council in heaven in Abraham, chapters 3, 4, and 5. The goal was to create man in the image of God, have him come to earth, give him free agency, teach him correct principles, have him prove that he will do all that God asks of him, and have him return, having grown intellectually and spiritually, redeemed with eternal life. Lucifer's plan was to accomplish the goal by taking away free agency, forcing us to live righteously and then taking all of the credit for insuring our salvation. Jesus stepped forward to obey the will of Heavenly Father. He said: 'Father, thy will be done, and the glory be thine forever.'[3] Our Father in Heaven chose Christ's model for achieving His goal of eternal life for mankind, and made him our Savior and Redeemer. Today we are each living out the result of that goal planning session.

"Another goal setting session occurred prior to the creation of the world. Can you imagine God, Christ, Adam and others setting a goal to

---

[3] Moses 4:2 *Pearl of Great Price*

create the universe, the earth, the plants, animals and even man, all in six days? Re-read Genesis and you'll catch a glimpse of this incredible goal oriented process.

"Soloman said, 'Where there is no vision, the people perish.' (Proverbs 29:18). Vision is the first part of a goal and is necessary to fulfill the measure of our creation, but it is only good with goals that demand action and actual accomplishments. Once two people understand even a portion of their missions on earth, they must translate those missions into goals that are specific and written, to drive the engine that will create what the Lord wants for them. A celestial marriage is not merely two people with individual goals and ideas who just happen to live together. It is the building of a glorious union, that has a purpose, which can only be realized through the efforts of those two individuals working together."

"But this just sounds like an extension of knowing your spouse's mission on earth, and supporting them to accomplish that mission," Jake admitted.

"That's right, Jake."

"But life's not that simple. Sometimes we're just given some difficult times. Goals don't keep us from experiencing them. Bad things happen."

"Right again, Jake, but it's what we do about the difficult times that matters, and goal setting can be a powerful part of the process. When Conrad and I were living in our 'leaky basement,' we reached a point where we had run out of food storage, and money. As a result, I had a spiritual experience in which I knew I had to get a job. Our goal had been to start our business and support ourselves with the proceeds, but it was taking longer than we had planned. So, the goal had to be modified a bit, with an emergency short-term goal to get our family on stable ground financially.

"We decided that I should start a ballet school. It was something I could do easily and set up quickly. All I needed were students and a place to teach. My girlfriend, Paula, was eager to help. She had an open house for all of her neighbors to meet me. They brought their children, and by the end of the get-together I had twenty students signed up for summer ballet school. Just as quickly, I had arranged to rent five hours a week of studio space from another ballet teacher.

"The night after everything was in place, I had a dream in which I saw myself teaching ballet to five students. Three of the students belonged to the other ballet teacher. As the class progressed, I suddenly heard a noise. The studio door opened, and in walked the other ballet teacher. She accused me of stealing three of her students, turned and walked out in a huff. Just then, the phone rang next to the bed, ending my dream and my very deep sleep. I had a 'whoosh' feeling from the Holy Spirit witness to me that the dream I had was from the Lord.

"Conrad answered the phone and handed it to me. It was the ballet teacher. She said that she had been thinking about our arrangement, and had decided that I would be too much competition for her. She said that she wouldn't let me rent the studio space from her after all. I just said, 'Okay. Goodbye.' I turned to Conrad and told him what had just transpired, including my dream. I told him also how glad I was that the Lord had warned me so I would not cry on the phone. Instead, I was calm and just knew it was meant to be. Conrad concurred and continued, 'That means that the Lord has something better for you, and I'm going to help you find it.'

"That very Saturday afternoon, we went out looking for another place to rent. Conrad, true to his word, drove me around day after day, until one morning we found an old American Legion Hall that had a small 'For Rent' sign in the window, with a telephone number. We called at a nearby phone booth. Within fifteen minutes, the President of that American Legion Post drove up in his car, unlocked the building, and led us into a spacious ballroom on the top floor. It was wonderful. We asked him how much it would cost a month. He said, 'Well, how much can you afford?' I hesitated, worried that my offer would be too low, and then continued knowing that I couldn't afford any more. 'I'm sorry but I can only afford seventy-five dollars a month.' He frowned as he looked at me, holding me in suspense. Then, to our utter astonishment, he offered, 'Oh no, that's way too much. We wouldn't want to charge you more than fifty dollars a month.' Was I hearing things or was this man crazy? No one in business ever says anything like that, *no one*.

"As we talked more, we found out that since the Viet Nam War, veterans weren't joining the American Legion because they were villainized so severely by the counter culture. The regular membership had moved away or died off to the point that their post had only three members remaining. They no longer could sustain the building, and were looking for someone to give it to.

"'Give it to?' My husband and I looked at each other and our hearts were beating fast. 'Yeah,' he continued, 'We are a non-profit organization, so we are looking for another non-profit organization to donate it to. We don't want to donate it to the Lions Club, who keep asking for it, because they will just sell the building and use the money for something else. This building means too much to us and we'd like to find someone who would serve the community in some way. Then, we'd transfer it to their non-profit organization.'

"We couldn't believe our ears. Conrad promised that he'd find me a studio with the help of the Lord. But, we never dreamed it might lead to actually owning a whole building, much less for free. We decided we would try to form a non-profit ballet company eligible to receive such a gift. Even if it didn't work out, it would be a good thing to do anyway. We rented the building, and I began teaching classes. Conrad figured out how to create a non-profit corporation in the state. He obtained our 501(c)(3) status from the Federal government. Its charter was for a children's ballet company that would perform classical ballets, and a 'special' ballet company.

"I had a soft spot in my heart for mentally retarded children. When I was growing up there were two mentally retarded girls in our ward. I loved them very much and I always felt badly that they didn't have all of the opportunities available to me. I thought how wonderful it would be to provide a free dance experience to mentally challenged children. So, we formed a side dance company, called The Pygmalion Dancers, for special kids. I planned to have the talented members of my ballet company take turns serving these children by volunteering to help teach them dance steps. It would serve two purposes: help the mentally retarded children have a great opportunity, and keep my talented dancers from developing 'swelled heads' due to their performance successes. By training The Pygmalion Dancers, my other students would learn the art of service to others.

"After putting this all together over a period of a few months, we presented the idea to the president of the American Legion Post. He was thrilled. Unknown to us, he and his wife had a mentally retarded child. He thought that having a ballet school and company in the community was a great idea, and even wanted his son to participate. He said he would take it before his group and the community leaders. Within a few days we received approval, and the American Legion Post officially donated the entire $150,000 building to us. What a gift from the Lord! And if it hadn't been for my partner in life, my teammate, it never would have happened. Another husband might have said, when the first studio rental fell through, 'Well, I guess you're not supposed to teach ballet after all.' Not my eternal partner, who has always been committed to seeing me achieve my potential on earth.

"Since the Lord gave me a building for free, I decided to dedicate it to the Lord. My father, mother, Conrad, our son Alexander and I went to the building, and my father offered a dedicatory prayer to the Lord. In the prayer I was blessed that the Lord would send some special spirits to me to teach, in whom I would be able to plant seeds of the gospel. And in time, some of them would join the church. What a wonderful promise! So far, one of my top ballerinas, Kim Pierce, who danced the lead role in Prokofiev's Cinderella Ballet, joined the church in 1996. She was married a year later in the Seattle Temple for time and all eternity. How joyous that occasion was!"

Jake looked as if he was giving in. "Okay, you've sort of convinced me that goal planning is important. But how do you get started? There are so many things to choose from."

"Yes, life is complex. But, I've found an easy way to break it up into manageable pieces. I divide my goals into the following categories: Spiritual, Family, Mental, Physical, Finance/Career, and Social. By setting goals in each one of these six areas, we can better achieve balance in our lives. If you focus too much on one area, you may actually cause problems in your life, because you're out of balance. It's like a man who becomes a bishop, and then spends all his time at church, sacrificing his family; or like a person who becomes an intellectual and spiritual giant, and then forgets to take care of his body. If he dies early of a heart attack, he'll miss putting his genius to any useful purpose. In addition to balance, you will want to make sure your goals sync up with your partner's, and that you have goals that you are working on together. There is a lot written about the mechanics of goal setting. Stephen Covey is my favorite author on the subject.

"It's also important that after we make these goals, we have faith that we can accomplish them. Then we must work as hard as we can to make them happen. We must endure the stretch in accomplishing something new. It takes practice to learn a new skill like playing the piano. It takes hard work and probably some pain to gain muscles from an aggressive exercise routine.

"Finally, we should pray to the Lord, asking Him to help us accomplish our goals. We should symbolically give up our goals to the Lord. He will help us."

Jake smiled wryly, "You've made your point. So what's our assignment this week?"

"You mean you were listening all that time your eyes were closed?"

"Don't push it. Just give us the assignment," he grumbled. "What I have to do to achieve perfection!"

Sarah and I burst into of laughter. Jake hesitated, and then joined us. I guess I had finally succeeded in reaching him.

ASSIGNMENT NUMBER FOUR:

Spend a day alone with your spouse to discuss, plan, and pray about your goals together. Then, write them out. Commit to an annual couple's goal setting session together. Set two or three goals in each of the following categories, and make sure you have a good balance among them.

---

1. SPIRITUAL

I

II

2. FAMILY

I

II

3. MENTAL

I

II

4. PHYSICAL

I

II

5. FINANCE/CAREER

I

II

6. SOCIAL

I

II

CHAPTER 5

THE GREAT GIFT OF FORGIVENESS AND ERASING PAST HURTS

To my delight, the following week, Sarah and Jake presented me with five pages of goals neatly organized and displayed in a brand new notebook. "It was actually fun," they expressed simultaneously. "Yeah, I'll look forward to doing this annually. Every year we'll see our progress, and have a little honeymoon in the bargain to boot," Jake explained.

"You mean I got you hooked?" I teased.

"Don't rub it in, coach. What's secret number five?"

"Secret number five for achieving a successful celestial marriage on earth is forgiveness. As celestial couples who are obeying the basic commandments of the Lord, we need to easily, freely and immediately forgive our spouse for any hurt they cause us."

"Did you hear that?" Jake asked Sarah. "She said that you are supposed to forgive me immediately!"

Sarah glared at Jake. She gritted her teeth and folded her arms across her chest. "Forgive *any* hurt?"

"We are not talking about abuse, or prolonged negative behavior. We eventually need to forgive those too. Some behavior is so severe that a marriage cannot continue. I am not talking about that kind of hurt."

"This is *not* my favorite subject," Sarah added.

"Hmm... Perhaps this is a problem in your marriage?"

"Problem?" Sarah's voice escalated in pitch.

"Sarah has a problem forgiving me," Jake explained.

"I have problems forgiving you? Right. And you're Mr. Perfect?"

I had obviously hit a nerve and needed a strategy. Neither one of them was receptive to advice, so I began our discussion with a story.

"One of my missionary companions, whom I will call Michelle, was a convert to the church at age nineteen. She exuded an enthusiasm about the gospel like no other. Her eyes sparkled when she talked about its principles, and her excitement was contagious. She was so successful in bringing people into the church in France, that I believe she probably broke every baptismal record of any missionary serving at the time. She was the embodiment of *joi de vivre,*(joy of life). Everybody loved her and she loved them.

"Michelle had grown up in the midst of the tumultuous 'Hippie Era.' She had experimented with drugs, run with a wild crowd, and fallen prey to the 'free love' philosophy. But, her pure soul always yearned for something better. So, when she was introduced to the gospel, she recognized it immediately as the truth. She was filled with a strong witness from the Holy Ghost that the Church of Jesus Christ of Latter-Day Saints was Christ's church on the earth.

"After a successful mission, she went to Brigham Young University. There she met a valiant returned missionary who fell madly in love with her. Michelle and Jim soon became engaged. They both had a witness from the Spirit that they were meant for each other. They made plans to be married in the temple for time and all eternity.

"Michelle began to think about her past. She knew that the Lord had forgiven her, but she wanted an open marriage relationship, with no secrets held back. Propelled by this inner thought, Michelle told Jim everything about her past. Jim listened carefully, and when she was through telling about all of her experiences and transgressions, he was in a state of shock. He was born in the church. He had lived a pure life, never straying from the commandments. He had always seen himself marrying a virgin. After all, he was a virgin, and had saved himself for his eternal mate. The pain overwhelmed him and he began to cry. He told Michelle that he was tremendously disturbed by her revelations. She began to cry too, and now wondered if she should have told him. He was confused and hurt, and questioned if he still wanted to marry her.

"Jim tried to explain how he felt. He said that he didn't want to feel the way he did, but he couldn't help it. After a difficult silence, they agreed to give themselves time apart to decide what they should do. Michelle spent several agonizing days alone, praying to the Lord. Jim did the same. When they were ready, Jim and Michelle reunited to talk about their future together. Michelle had prayed that the Lord would bless her to say what He wanted her to say to Jim, and that whatever was meant to happen, would. Michelle began, 'If only I had grown up with the gospel like you did, Jim. Then we wouldn't be in this situation.

I always had a longing for the Spirit in my heart, and it took me a long time to find it. I would do anything if I could be a virgin for you. I would do anything to erase my past, but I can't. *But Jesus Christ can, and he did.'*

"Her words penetrated deeply into Jim's heart. He turned to her and said, 'Then I can do no less.' Her words made him know that he, too, could erase her past. Suddenly, he had a personal witness of the true meaning of forgiveness. He drew her close to him, and gave her a powerful hug filled with love from the depths of his soul.

"This story is a model of forgiveness. We can look at our spouse when we feel hurt by each other, and remember that the Lord has already forgiven them for whatever hurt they have caused us. Then we can say, as Jim did, 'I can do no less.'"

Sarah huffed, "You make it sound like it should be so easy to forgive each other and it's really not like that."

"I'm not saying that forgiveness is easy. But, it is necessary. There are almost always two sides to everything. We are all imperfect. We all make mistakes. Just as being imperfect is universal, the need for unconditional forgiveness is also universal. Fault moves from one person to another and back again."

"She always thinks that it's my fault," Jake added dolefully.

"It's not uncommon for one partner in a marriage to blame nearly everything that goes wrong on their companion. And yet, it is almost never the case that only one person deserves all the blame. We need to know and understand that most of the time, both partners contribute to the problem."

"I don't believe that," Sarah replied.

"Let me ask you this question: In the case of adultery, do you think that the person who committed the sin is the only one at fault?"

Sarah paused and then answered, aware that she might be getting herself into a trap. "Yes. It's black and white. The person who committed the sin was the evil one, and the spouse that was wronged is innocent."

"Is this true? Do you agree?" I looked at Jake for an opinion.

He shrugged his shoulders, appearing too tired to think.

"In most cases, adultery is only an overt manifestation of many underlying problems brewing in a marriage."

"How so?" Jake perked up.

"Are you ready for another story? It will illustrate my point." They both nodded.

"There is a woman I admire tremendously. I shall call her Lois. Her husband was in a prominent leadership position in the church. Everyone admired him. Then one day, while he was out of town on a business trip, he committed adultery with one of his colleagues. Steeped in guilt, he readily confessed his sin to the bishop. He was immediately released from his leadership position and excommunicated from the Church.

"Lois was a model of forgiveness. She never criticized her husband. Instead, she stood by him. She asked her husband what it was that she had done to help cause this moral transgression. She listened to his needs. She lost weight. She repented of her own selfishness and neglect of her husband. Over time, she learned to give him the kind of love that he was lacking. Together, and with the help of the Lord, they solved the underlying problems that had eroded the foundation of their marriage.

"Friends and acquaintances observed her actions with amazement. She completely forgave her husband, only thinking the best of him. She only cared about one thing: solving the problems that had helped push him over the edge and into moral transgression. He, too, was humble and addressed the issues that had brought them to this difficult point in their marriage. He begged for forgiveness from her, and worked as hard as he could to resolve every problem in their marriage. He wanted to achieve a oneness, and so did Lois.

"Today, they are a model of happiness and service in the church. Because of the great gift of forgiveness to her husband, and his willingness to repent and work at solving the problems in their marriage, they are now on the road to achieving a celestial marriage on earth."

"I don't understand what the wife did that was so wrong? So what if she gained weight?" Sarah looked perplexed.

"The weight issue was minor. The real problem was complex. Let me explain. Lois went through a difficult time giving birth to their third child. She was overwhelmed with diapers, night feedings, three children under the age of six, and having to go back to work part time to support the family. She was exhausted most of the time, and couldn't give to one more person by the time she went to bed. At first it was two weeks. Then, the weeks stretched into months. At last, one year had gone by without making love."

"Yikes. That would be tough," Jake added.

"Yes it was. And Lois was also unhappy with her marriage. She felt like everybody's servant. No one, including her husband, was giving her the kind of love that she needed?"

"What did she need?" Jake asked, genuinely.

Sarah slapped him on the back teasingly. "Isn't it just like a man not to get it?"

"Okay, Miss Know-It-All. You tell me what she needed," Jake challenged.

"In the first place, I bet they weren't having a weekly date. Am I right?" Sarah looked at me hopefully.

Her insight tickled me. I was delighted that *The Five Pillars of a Celestial Marriage* were prominent in her mind. "Bingo," I exclaimed.

"I knew it!" Sarah triumphed, jumping up from the couch. "No dates, no romance. Simple. I bet they didn't have daily talk time either, because if they had, they would have discussed the problem."

"What problem?" Jake shouted. "I still don't see what a weekly date, or talk time has to do with sex?"

Sarah emitted a guttural sound from her vocal cords that indicated her contempt. "Look Bub, you're just lucky you married me, and not Lois, or you might end up in the same trap." A guilty expression swept across Sarah's face. "I'm sorry, Jake. I didn't mean to put you down. It's just that some men take women for granted."

"Sarah's right," I added in an attempt to rescue her. "Some men do not try to give their mate the kind of love that they need. And, sex is an important part of giving love to another in marriage. Sex for many women can be more about giving pleasure to their husband than receiving pleasure in return. Because a woman doesn't always have an orgasm like a man, over the years, lovemaking can turn into a regular act of service. Once a mutual romantic manifestation of love, sex can become a chore when pleasure is only one sided."

"Hold on there! Sounds like you're making women out to be martyrs."

"Sometimes they are. Lois felt like a martyr. After an exhausting day coping with the children and juggling a part time job, she still had to prepare the dinner, give the children baths, read nighttime stories and tuck them in. As if that wasn't enough, she needed to finish the laundry and iron her husband's shirts for the week. She wanted to go to bed to sleep. Having sex with her husband meant even more mental energy if she was to experience any pleasure herself. If only her husband had given her understanding for her difficult burdens, and given her some help with the children. Instead, night after night she would look at the clock and think, 'It's almost eleven. I've got to get up at six. I need eight hours of sleep. There isn't time.' This pattern gets old. Hence, a year had passed since they had been intimate with each other. His needs were not fulfilled and he succumbed to temptation. The devastating result was adultery."

Jake contested. "We are all frantic with work, family, church, service. Who has time to always act like you're on a honeymoon?"

"That's another reason dates are so important. A woman needs to feel valued and appreciated. She needs romance. If you have a weekly date, you can set aside a quantity of time for quality intimacy. A man needs romance too, or he'll be tempted to look elsewhere. The result of a weekly date is self-evident. Remember, adultery is a two-way street."

"Sounds like you are making excuses for adultery," Jake expounded.

"I'm merely pointing out that any problem in a marriage is usually caused by two people, not just one. Rarely is there an absolute saint or an absolute villain in a marriage."

Sarah pursed her lips together and stood up to stretch and think. "You've told a story of forgiveness that illustrates an extreme case. Most of us don't have to forgive something so serious."

"That's right, Sarah. Instead, we let little irritating habits of our mate pull us down to a telestial level in a marriage."

"Now we're getting someplace," Jake interrupted. "This is our problem. The other day Sarah got mad at me because I invited my family over for breakfast on Sunday, just before my brother gave his returned missionary talk in sacrament meeting."

"Well, he didn't ask me. He just told me," Sarah complained.

"What's wrong with that, Jake?" I asked.

"Yeah, well, now I know that I should have asked her what she thought. We should have discussed it and then made the decision together."

"Good," I smiled.

"Not good. No matter how many times I have apologized, she won't forgive me," Jake moaned.

"Oh, you make me so mad! You're not telling the whole story," Sarah countered.

"What?"

"As if you don't know. You see? This is just what's wrong."

"She does this all the time to me. I never know why I'm in the dog house."

"Okay, you two! Sarah, explain exactly what happened step by step after he invited his folks over for breakfast."

"Well, we didn't have anything in the refrigerator. I would have gone to Costco to get enough food if I had known. That was the first thing that really angered me. I like to be prepared."

"Didn't I offer to help you?"

"Trouble number two. Jake starts helping me cook breakfast. My in laws are walking around and they hear him telling me what to do. 'Flip the pancakes now,' he said. I could have kicked him. I know how to cook. The whole thing was embarrassing for me."

"Jake, did you tell her that you were sorry?" I asked.

"Yes, over and over, but she won't forgive me," Jake lamented.

"Why? Sarah," I asked.

"Because I want him to suffer," She said.

"Why?" I asked, mystified.

"He can't just say 'sorry' and it's all better. I need time."

"What do you mean?" I probed.

"Well what I really want is for him to understand my feelings, not just toss it off like it didn't matter."

"You mean that he doesn't listen to you?"

"Yeah. I want him to understand how he hurt me. I want him to feel what I felt and then tell me he's sorry. Then I'd believe him and be able to forgive him," Sarah offered.

"Did you get that Jake?" I asked.

"Yeah. I'm supposed to listen to her complain, and go on for hours about how I wronged her."

"See!" Sarah said grudgingly. "He doesn't want to do it."

Jake answered. "You got that right. Why should I sit there and listen to you rub my nose in the dirt, and tell me over and over what a deficient husband I am?"

"Is that so much to ask when you hurt her first?" I asked.

"Ouch," He replied. "I guess you got me there."

"After you have hurt a person and tell them that you're sorry, they need to have an opportunity to tell you how you hurt them. They have to get the poison you fed them out of their system. Then, true forgiveness can be forthcoming. They need to know that you are sincerely sorry. You show that by listening to them, and putting yourself in their shoes. If they feel that you truly understand their point of view, then, and only then, is your 'sorry' a true sign of remorse, and a commitment to never repeat that offense again."

"Jake, she's right. I feel that if I forgive you, that it's just a license to do it again. What she's saying is exactly what I want to hear from you," Sarah said.

"Everyone wants to hear phrases like, 'I had no idea you felt that way. I'm so sorry. I can imagine how you feel now, and I would feel the same way, too, if you had done to me what I did to you. Do you think you can find it in your heart to forgive me?'"

Jake's eyes began to sparkle. "Well, I don't know if I can put that many words together at one time. And, I can't guarantee that I won't make the same mistake again. But, I do see what you're saying. Let me try." He turned to Sarah and held her hand. "Sarah, I promise you that from this day forth, I will always listen to your feelings when I hurt you. I will listen with understanding so that you know that I really love you, care about you, and mean it when I say 'I'm sorry.'"

Sarah let go of his hand and put her arms around her husband. They embraced for a long poignant moment. Finally, they parted and Sarah wiped a tear from her eye. Jake heaved a heavy sigh.

"That's wonderful," I observed. "I hope you both have many more moments like this in your marriage. These are *celestial moments* when you catch a glimpse of what a marriage can be.

"Now, I'd like to talk for a few minutes about another aspect of forgiveness. It involves criticism and the little flaws we all have. Truly, we have to differentiate between what is important and what is not. We need to think about what can be changed and what cannot. My mother gave me excellent words of advice as I was dating. She said, 'Never marry someone with the idea that you are going to change him. You can't. Accept the man you marry for who he is; then love him and never criticize him. If he improves on some of his faults over the years, consider yourself married to an extraordinary man. On the other hand, if he stays the same, faults and all, you will have married him knowing his weaknesses, and knowing that you accepted him *as is*.' This philosophy makes for great love between a man and woman because criticism is eliminated, and forgiveness of minor flaws is given in advance.

"I am always mystified by husbands and wives who think that they must be completely candid, when their mate asks for their opinion. For example, an overweight friend of mine asked her husband how he liked her new dress. He, being an *always-tell-the-truth-even-if-it-hurts-person*, said, 'It makes you look fat. You need to lose weight before you'll look good in anything.' How cruel! In the guise of being truthful, he hurt his wife tremendously. Maybe she is overweight. But she didn't ask him what she already knew in her heart. She asked him if he liked the dress. Was this husband really telling the truth?" I asked.

"No," Sarah blurted out. "He was stating his opinion. He wasn't being forgiving of his wife's individual weakness. Besides, maybe a man in Italy would be mad for this lady's plumpish figure. The Renaissance painters seemed to like overweight women!"

Laughing, Jake added, "Trust me when I say that not all men like bone-thin women."

"That's right. And as for the dress, taste is in the eye of the beholder. So truth can be relative when it comes to beauty and fashion. It's only a matter of opinion. The real issue here is that this man, when he criticized his wife, was showing his intolerance of her current weakness. He was demonstrating a classic lack of love and forgiveness, a withholding of the greatest gifts we can give our mate."

"But this doesn't remove our desire to change our husband or wife. What do we do about that?" Jake asked solemnly.

"Jake, I know this is difficult, because it seems to go against our natural instincts to try to improve each other through criticism. But, remember, the one place on earth that a person should feel safe from harm is at home with an eternal companion. Criticism tears us apart and has no place in a celestial marriage. I'm not saying that we should lie to our companion. I'm saying that we should be careful so that we don't hurt them. You can't change anyone. Only they can do it themselves. Just be ready when they ask you for help."

"So, what should that man have said to his wife?" Jake asked.

By the way she interrupted, you could tell that Sarah relished these kinds of questions. She answered, "Jake, you would say: 'Wow, I can tell that you love the dress. You sparkle in it.'"

Jake and I laughed at her tactful, but truthful statement.

"The bottom line is that we should never criticize something that we cannot change ourselves. It was obvious that his wife thought it was a beautiful dress or she wouldn't have purchased it. No doubt she was hoping that it would appeal to her husband. If, on the other hand, she really wanted his opinion about the dress, he should have only answered her question - how he felt about the dress, and avoided any comments outside the question. She was already aware of the fact that she was overweight, and probably more sensitive to it than anyone could imagine. We usually know our faults only too well. His negative statement would not only hurt her feelings, but might even increase her problem by making her want to eat even more."

Sarah interrupted again. "That's right. The wife never asked for an opinion about her weight. What she really needed at that moment was a little love and understanding."

"Exactly. What difference would it make in the eternities of time if the husband liked the dress? None. What mattered was the kind of love he gave her at that moment. We can scar people for life by one negative statement. By being intolerant and unforgiving of our mate's foibles, we commit the greater sin.

"In the *Doctrine and Covenants*, chapter 64, verses 8-10, it says: 'My disciples, in days of old, sought occasion against one another and forgave not one another in their hearts; and for this evil they were afflicted and sorely chastened. Wherefore, I say unto you, that ye ought to forgive one another; for he that forgiveth not his brother his trespasses standeth condemned before the Lord; for there remaineth in him the greater sin. I, the Lord, will forgive whom I will forgive, but of you it is required to forgive all men.'"

"That's profound," Jake contributed. "Explicit, in fact. We are required to forgive everyone!"

"Yes, everyone. And most of all, shouldn't we freely forgive our spouse, the person with whom we plan to spend eternity? I believe the answer is a resounding 'yes.' Forgiveness should be given freely. Otherwise, we are under the greater condemnation. The Lord further expresses that we will bring afflictions upon ourselves. This concept alone is motivation to forgive my spouse. However, for me, I want to forgive my husband freely because I want him to forgive me for all my faults and imperfections.

"Of course, the ultimate example of forgiveness we have is in the death of our Lord and Master. When Jesus was hanging on the cross and bearing up under the extreme pain of a long and torturous death, he still uttered the famous words, 'Father, forgive them, for they know not what they do.' (Luke 23:34). This depth of perfection is what we are all striving to achieve.

"One of my glamorous friends, early in her life, dated a fellow for several months. He told her that no matter what she did, she could never be sexy to a man. Even though she was attractive, she believed what he said was true. It really hurt her. No matter how often her friends told her she was pretty, she didn't believe them. She married someone else a few years later. During their talk time, she told her husband about this hurtful statement. He replied, 'Who was he? Give me his name and I'll take care of him.' She started laughing. Then he continued, 'Don't you know he was manipulating you? He knew that if he could make you feel badly about yourself, he could get you to do anything he wanted. He just wanted to get you into bed. Fortunately, you were too smart to fall for his reverse psychology.' This marvelous husband managed to erase, in a few sentences, a statement that had haunted her for years. He demonstrated the difference between love and selfishness."

"I'm happy to say this is one area where Sarah and I are right on track. I've always felt like I was too thin. You know, it's a male thing. I don't have a muscular chest in spite of the fact that I've been lifting weights for ten years, and I work out at the gym daily. It's not in my genetics to look like Arnold Schwartzenegger. When I ask Sarah if she thinks I look like a weakling, she always tells me that she prefers a body type like mine!"

Sarah smiled and raised her eyebrows, proud that she had done something right in their marriage. "This is one principle that we've perfected. There is nothing that can be done about physical imperfections."

"One could argue that plastic surgery can remedy certain defects." Sarah replied. "Yeah, but who can afford it? Anyway, it shouldn't be necessary. You married the person because you were attracted to them."

"One of my girlfriends obsessed about her nose. When she asked her boyfriend if he thought her nose was too misshapen, he replied, 'It adds to your whole image. How can I isolate one feature of an extremely attractive woman? I love you just the way you are, and I wouldn't change a thing.'"

Jake commented. "Smart man. Way to win a woman's heart."

"And keep it," Sarah said as if she had just scored another debate point.

"We have to forgive things that don't matter. When a husband or wife puts on weight, it's better to forgive this imperfection. After all, we have faults too. *Quid pro quo.* Overlooking faults and forgiving them is part of the foundation of a celestial marriage.

"I counseled a couple that had taken my Celestial Marriage class twice. The husband still doesn't understand this concept. He continues to harp on the same faults he finds in his wife. At one of their goal setting sessions together, his wife suggested they start a missionary fund for a mission together after the children were launched on their own. All he could say was, 'I only have one goal, and that's for you to lose weight.' My heart ached as I heard him. How could he be so blind to his own faults? He was chronically disheveled and often went several days without shaving. He failed to see what a beautiful soul he had married. She had a gift for teaching and was raising her children to love the Lord.

"This man's failure to forgive his wife's inability to stay thin prevented him from attaining a celestial marriage on earth. As the years peeled away, they argued more and more, and bitterness built up thick walls of unhappiness around both of them. Sarah, Jake, what could he have done differently?"

"He could have forgiven her for her weakness of overeating, and he should have focused on changing his own faults and imperfections," Jake responded.

"If only he had focused on developing the fundamentals of a celestial marriage."

Sarah remarked, "You know they didn't practice the *Five Pillars of a Celestial Marriage.*"

"Yeah. They probably didn't have a couple's nightly prayer, or a weekly date or daily talk time."

"Or scripture reading and a weekly planning meeting," Sarah added.

I continued. "If they had just followed these five simple principles, they would have found such joy together. It is virtually impossible not to forgive each other when we are reporting in to the Lord each night. Personally, as I kneel down with my husband in the sanctity of our bedroom, it suddenly transposes itself into our own private temple. We literally envision ourselves kneeling before the Lord. I can see Him in my mind. And, as we pray, I want to be one with my husband. There is no way that I want to face the Lord, loaded with petty differences between my husband and me. I know that the Lord loves my husband and forgives him freely. How can I do any less?"

"I want to be forgiving of Sarah on little habits, but I confess that they sometimes really get to me. What should I do?"

"What do I do that bothers you?" Sarah asked defensively.

"We don't need to talk about that right now," I advised. "Save it for your talk time tonight and use these small things to practice on. First of all, Jake, you must concentrate on the good points in Sarah, not the negative ones. Think about supporting her in her goals, and the mutual goals you have as a couple. We have the power to control our minds. We can think whatever we want. If we think about the positive, we will progress upwards towards celestial behavior. If we think negatively, we will experience unhappiness and spiral downward towards the telestial. When we forgive and forget, always thinking the best of each other, we are, in essence, practicing an unconditional love just as Christ exemplified on earth.

"Naturally, there are negative behaviors that each one of us need to change along the eternal pathway to perfection. Our mates can support us in these changes. But, these changes must be born in those who need to change. A goal to change must be their idea, not ours. We should first seek to change ourselves, not our mates. I love the story in the New Testament about the townsfolk who wanted to stone an adulterous woman. Christ came up to the crowd and uttered the poignant statement, 'He that is without sin among you, let him first cast a stone at her.' (John 8:7). In shame, they all slunk away.

"While I was serving a mission in France, I was given a companion with whom I had nothing in common but the gospel. She was irritating to me in every way. She criticized my love of ballet, theater and the arts. She had no desire on *Preparation Day* to explore the ancient castles and learn about the history and culture of France. To her, these architectural wonders were nothing more than piles of rubble. After trying for two months to love her and find common ground, my patience had worn thin. One night as we turned out the lights and knelt down on opposite sides of our Louis XV antique double bed we had to share, I began to pray. I was planning on complaining to the Lord about this intolerable companion. Suddenly, I felt prompted to open my eyes. I looked at her silhouette kneeling in prayer. I thought how ironic it was that we were both praying to the Lord at the same time. We were both on missions serving the Lord. And, she was probably praying to the Lord, on the other side of the bed, complaining about me, the artsy city girl that she couldn't stand. I closed my eyes again, and changed my prayer. I told the Lord that I knew He loved her just as much as me. She was sacrificing just like me. She loved the Gospel just like me. She was a special daughter of our Heavenly Father just like me. I knew that God loved her so much. How could I do any less? From then on, I focused on all of her wonderful qualities, and I ended up with a great love and appreciation for her. This was another experience and lesson I shall never forget.

"We must see each other as the Lord sees us. We must remember that when we cease to forgive, we are insulting our Father in Heaven. He loves our spouse just as much as He loves us. And that's the bottom line.

"When we are married in the temple for time and all eternity, we kneel across the altar from each other while incredible covenants are made and blessings promised. We hold each other's hand symbolizing that we are marrying into the eternal bond of forgiveness. I can still remember Conrad holding my hand in a special way, as if I was a character in a movie, who suddenly experiences a flashback, and now sees life with new eyes. It is a major self-revelation to understand that forgiveness is a central concept in eternal marriage."

Jake and Sarah looked at each other, and then at me. The expression on their faces indicated enlightenment. They understood what I was talking about.

"In the seventies there was a very popular movie starring Ali McGraw and Ryan O'Neil called *Love Story*. It was about two hip college students who attended Ivy League schools. The girl made a statement in the movie that became its theme, and was highlighted on every movie poster: 'Love means never having to say you're sorry.' I despise this philosophy! It is the antithesis of true love. When you really love someone, you say 'I'm sorry' often and without regard to who's right and who's wrong. Love is being humble enough to not have to always be the one who's right. Love is being able to say you're sorry, and mean it because you value your marriage more than your ego.

"What happens when we don't forgive our mates? We stunt our own growth and our spouse's growth. When Conrad and I married, we became friends with an outstanding couple. I will call them Sherry and Vic. They were destined for greatness. She was the Relief Society President of our ward, and he was the Gospel Doctrine teacher. Vic had already been in a bishopric, and was a leader in every way. He had a promising career and was moving up the ladder in the corporate world. Sherry was a terrific mother, and could have been classified as a *Super Mom*. She could paint, play the piano beautifully, and had been a state beauty pageant winner. Vic looked the part of a handsome, Hollywood leading man. They wowed and dazzled everyone. What a couple!

"Having similar interests, we formed a dinner group with them and several other couples. We were the newlyweds of the group. At the time, I didn't notice the signs of their eroding marriage. During our dinner parties, Vic would make sarcastic remarks about Sherry. I remember being stunned. Conrad and I had only been married for three months, and we were so enamored by each other that we couldn't believe anyone married in the temple would put their mate down in public.

"To make a long story short, a few years later, Vic committed adultery. Sherry immediately moved out with the children, without any thought of forgiving her husband, or asking him what she might have done to contribute to his sin. She didn't even ask, 'How can we rescue our relationship, and return to the celestial marriage track?' She immediately filed for divorce, which ended miserably for all involved. Sherry remarried two more times, never finding happiness. Now she is single, and living a lifestyle accepted only in the world. Vic was excommunicated. He never stopped attending church faithfully, in spite of the humiliation. He knew the church was true. On his third marriage, he found happiness, and was rebaptized into the church. His story is one of true forgiveness from the Lord, and endurance to learn how to live the gospel principles.

"Vic's rebaptism was a joyous experience. When he was confirmed a member of the church, and received the Gift of Holy Ghost, what followed will forever stay in my mind. He was told during the blessing that his mission on earth had now been altered. He was told that he only had one responsibility remaining before he returned to his Father in Heaven, and that was to learn how to have a celestial marriage on earth.

"The words penetrated my soul profoundly. They were meaningful in a personal way. I knew that although I had many things to accomplish for the Lord, first and foremost was my responsibility to learn how to have a celestial marriage on earth. If it was true for Vic, and for me, it must be true for everyone. In other words, for most of us, marriage is the most important thing we do on earth."

"A while back in our conversation, you said that we should always think the best of our spouse," Jake ventured.

"That's right. When my husband does something that I don't like, something minor, I say. 'That is so unlike you. Usually, you are so considerate. I know you didn't mean to hurt me.'"

"I like that. I wish you'd feel that way about me, Sarah," Jake said.

"I'm learning," Sarah responded.

"I have friends whose children can do no wrong. If their child is in a fight with other children, they will assuredly blame the other child. They insist that their child is giving, loving, and would never hurt anyone. Although I really dislike the fact that they cannot see reality, this quality is actually marvelous in a celestial marriage. If we would only express such thoughts as: 'It's okay, honey, I know you would never hurt me on purpose.' It is looking through kind eyes; it is giving the benefit of the doubt; it is never saying such things as, 'you always forget,' or 'you always make that same mistake.' It is, instead, seeing an offense as an exception to a pattern of loving behavior usually apparent in your mate.

"My husband used to have a habit of making up silly, nonsensical words to music when he couldn't remember the lyrics. To him, it was funny. But, I didn't like it. It drove me crazy. It finally got to me one day, and I remember responding sarcastically, 'You need to go to a linguistics and memory school.' I was ashamed of myself for saying such a thing. I realized that it was not the way I would want Conrad to talk to me. As I pondered the situation, I remembered that this behavior was a habit he had learned in his home. Suddenly in my mind I could separate this behavior from the man. It wasn't his fault that he was taught this habit in his home.

"After realizing that we are all the product of our upbringing, and we may develop little habits that will be irritating to others, I thought about some of my faults. I once developed a terrible habit of shaking in bed. It was my version of rocking myself to sleep. To Conrad it resembled an earthquake. I was hoping it would be appealing to him, like being in a vibrating bed. No such luck. I didn't succumb to this habit every night, but frequently enough to be annoying. My kind husband merely stated that it bothered him, and he was sure there was a solution that would satisfy both of us. In researching vitamin therapy he found that I was deficient in certain minerals. Now I drink cranberry juice combined with minerals each night before I go to bed. Voila! I don't shake any more. His approach assumed that it wasn't my fault. Rather than complain, he decided to solve the problem for me. We laugh about it now."

Sarah and Jake laughed uncontrollably. "Are you sure that you didn't make up that story?" Jake questioned.

"You'll never know, will you?"

"Ah, come on. Was that true?"

"Yes it was. Where do you think comedy writers get their material? From real-life situations, of course.

"When you think about your own foibles, you realize that everyone has them. Now I laugh off most of my husband's irritating habits and say to myself, 'It isn't his fault. It's his family's fault.' Then, I feel an outpouring of love towards my husband who has to deal with my imperfections!

"Today we have talked about two levels of forgiveness in a marriage. The first involves the breaking of major commandments. It necessitates profound expressions of forgiveness, and involves an intense commitment to work through it together. The second level of forgiveness involves character flaws and hurts. In spite of seeming insignificance, some of these can actually be the inciting event that eventually destroys a marriage. These are the things that we must forgive on a daily basis.

"Forgiveness is allowing your spouse the freedom to grow, learn, and progress onward toward perfection. Our marital unit is the perfect design of God, and the best way we have of learning to become like God. 'Be ye therefore perfect, even as your Father which is in Heaven is perfect.' (Matthew 5: 48)."

Jake beamed. "Now, I understand more than ever that marriage is an incredible way to achieve perfection. Learning to forgive each other and a willingness to change ourselves is what constitutes a happy marriage."

Sarah added, "Yeah, it's like when we marry in the temple, we marry into the atonement of Christ, a perfect model of forgiveness, the foundation of being able to perfect ourselves in a marriage."

"That's right. With constant forgiveness from the Lord and our mate, in a safe place where we can practice becoming a better person, we can actually develop a celestial marriage on earth."

Sarah raised her head and looked me straight in the eyes. "I want specifics. How do I forgive and forget? We've already talked about Jake listening to me. But what else should we do?"

I reached into my valise and pulled out two handouts I frequently use in my Celestial Marriage class. "Not to worry, I have a summary all written down for you here. Shall we read it together?" They nodded and I read out loud.

HOW TO FORGIVE AND FORGET
(can be done alone or with one's spouse)

1. Start with a prayer. Ask your Father in Heaven to inspire you and help you to complete the act of forgiveness.
2. Write down the offending action and how it made you feel, or simply tell your spouse in person. The offender should listen without interrupting, and exercise understanding and sympathy.
3. Explain or write down why you think your partner did what he or she did.
4. Explain or write down anything that you did to contribute to the offense.
5. Put the offense in perspective by seeing it as an event in the eternities of time.
6. Verbalize or make a list recounting all of your partner's good points.
7. Review your individual missions in life, and your missions together. Write down how you are supporting each other.
8. Tell you partner that you forgive him or her completely.
9. Kneel and pray together.
10. Do something with or for your partner to create new memories. (A romantic date, make him a surprise, bring her flowers, quality talk time, etc.)
11. Never bring the offense up again. *Never.* Be like the Lord who forgives and remembers no more.
12. Let time pass to heal the hurt.

IF YOU STILL CAN'T FORGIVE YOUR MATE, PROCEED TO:

THE EIGHT STEP PROGRAM OF FORGIVENESS

1. List your faults or deficiencies on paper, such as: can't cook, can't sew, can't repair a car, can't repair things around the house, antisocial, a little lazy, critical, a spender, impulsive, etc.
2. List the sins for which you have asked the Lord to forgive you, such as: intolerance, judging others, selfishness, impure thoughts, lying,

thoughtlessness, etc.

3. List your bad habits that your mate has to live with, such as: leaving a messy bathroom, eating and dropping crumbs all over the couch, biting your fingernails, etc.

4. Pray to the Lord, thanking him for the wonderful mate you have who puts up with your imperfections. Then, ask the Lord to forgive you for being harsh on your mate.

5. Ask the Lord to erase any bad feelings you have toward your spouse and ask Him to help you see only his or her good points.

6. Envision Christ who said, while he was dying on the cross, "Father, forgive them for they know not what they do." (Luke 23:34).

7. Remember Father in Heaven loves your mate just as much as He does you.

8. Remember, if you don't forgive your mate for the hurts he or she has caused, you are disobeying a commandment from the Lord! Think about it. "Wherefore, I say unto you, that ye ought to forgive one another, for he that forgiveth not his brother his trespasses standeth condemned before the Lord; for there remaineth in him the greater sin. I, the Lord, will forgive whom I will forgive, but of you it is required to forgive all men." (D&C 64:9-10). You must forgive and forget. For in this ability lies the gift of true love and celestial marriage on earth.

"This is great," Sarah offered. "I'll tape them up on my mirror."

"Yes, that's a good idea. And also, always remember to think the best of your partner. Make it a habit to be positive and say words like: 'That is so unlike you. You would never do anything like that. What happened? I understand. It's okay, I know that you really love me. Of course, I forgive you. I've made so many mistakes, how could I not forgive you, when you and the Lord have been so forgiving of me. I know you'll never do that again.'

"The antithesis of a positive attitude towards your mate is always thinking the worst and blaming them. 'How could you do that to me? You are always so inconsiderate. You always make me late. You never think of anyone but yourself. You are so selfish.' These statements never address the problem directly. They infer that your mate is hopeless and always going to be that way."

"That's great, but what about me? You know, the one who always makes the mistake in our marriage," Jake expressed facetiously. "What am I supposed to do, besides listen and understand Sarah's point of view? Have another handout, teach?" Jake asked.

"As a matter of fact," I reached into my valise and produced another paper. "Voila!"

IF YOU ARE THE ONE WHO OFFENDED:

1. Listen to your mate non-defensively. Allow them to explain how you hurt them. Seek to understand their position. Repeat what they say and ask them if that's how they see it. Truly empathize with them.

2. Say you're sorry and ask for their forgiveness.

3. Promise them that you won't repeat the mistake again. Then, never do it again, no matter what. Sincerely seek to overcome the mistake.

4. Seek to replace your mistake with a positive behavior that will give love to your mate.

5. Thank your mate for forgiving you, and emphasize how much you need their help to overcome this habit or mistake. Tell them that you really appreciate their patience and love.

"Okay, you two. Now tell me, what do we want from our mate when we've made a mistake, and have asked for forgiveness?"

Sarah and Jake stared back at me. "You tell us, Maestro."

"We want them to forgive us easily and express their love to us. It is a dreadful response when a spouse, who has been hurt, vindictively withdraws love. It is a form of retaliation. In some cases, the offender will practically crawl on their hands and knees, begging for forgiveness, until the person offended feels that their partner has begged and suffered enough to warrant forgiveness. This is totally opposite of Christ-like forgiveness.

"If you are praying together nightly while holding hands and truly reporting in to the Lord as partners, forgiveness really becomes easier. When our spouse hurts us, we should first ask them the question, 'What did I do to contribute to this problem?' Suddenly, forgiveness will become a team effort, rather than an individual effort."

Without saying one word, Sarah put out her hand, indicating that she wanted the next assignment. Tears were rolling down her cheeks. She leaned over to embrace Jake. "I'm so sorry for all of the times I've been so hard on you, and haven't forgiven you right away. Please forgive me. I love you so much."

Jake whispered. "Oh honey. I forgive you. You are just about perfect in every way. I just have to learn how to love you more, and in the way you want to be loved."

The scene was touching – my cue to leave. I exited without any fanfare. My work was done for the day.

ASSIGNMENT NUMBER FIVE:

1. Review all the hand outs. Memorize the steps of forgiving and asking for forgiveness. Then, implement them in your life.
2. Use your talk time to work on the especially difficult areas where forgiveness has been a problem.
3. Make a commitment to each other that you will never let a day go by without forgiving each other.
4. Review the following examples of hurts we may cause and how to overcome them.

PROBLEM: Your spouse talks about you negatively in front of others.

SOLUTION: During talk time, ask if you can discuss a situation that hurts you. Express to your mate that you are hurt by these public comments. You know you're not perfect, but it hurts deeply to hear your faults discussed with others. Ask why he or she does it? Ask him or her if he or she is getting enough love from you? Ask what you can do? Usually, when we criticize others in public, it is because our own self-esteem is low and we want praise from others. By criticizing someone else, it somehow boosts our feelings about ourselves. We put the other person down, hoping to increase our status with thoughts like: "I'm a better person. I don't do that!" Seek to find a solution together. Perhaps this would be a great Christmas gift: promising not to put your spouse down in public again.

PROBLEM: Your spouse is inconsiderate of you in some way, such as forgetting to clean up after a bath, forgetting to mail a letter for you, forgetting to pick up the shirts at the laundry, being one hour late to pick you up for a date, from work, etc.

SOLUTION: The one who has been neglected or hurt should first and foremost assume the best. Statements like this go a long way: "I see you forgot to clean up after yourself. Was that the night you were late for your bishopric meeting? I knew it. You're usually so considerate. Did you forget to stop at the laundry? I understand. I've been preoccupied too. It's just lucky that I can eke another day out of today's shirt. So, I'll just put on a heavy dose of cologne!" (Then laugh. Laughter is the salve that heals the wound.) "I'm so glad to see you! I was starting to worry that you had been in an accident. Are you okay? What happened?"

A dear friend of mine named Tom set a great example for me. One time we were walking down the street together and a good friend walked by. Tom called out, "Hi Alan." Alan totally ignored him and walked away. I would have been hurt; but Tom wasn't. He said, "Oh, he must have had something on his mind. It's not like him. He's such a caring friend." This was just one of many examples of Tom's forgiving spirit. He always thought the best of everyone. That is what Father in Heaven wants us to do when thinking about our spouse. Think the best of them, and believe that they would never try to hurt us purposely.

PROBLEM: Your mate fails to act as your best friend and confidant. Example: One day you are very upset with an event that has occurred, and you need a shoulder to cry on. Your husband or wife doesn't have time for you. Or, they listen and do not show any understanding because they are preoccupied with their own troubles.

SOLUTION: Assume the best. Later that day, talk about the event calmly, and ask if your mate was having a hard day, too. Be understanding, and talk about your feelings. Forgive before they ask for forgiveness.

PROBLEM: A husband goes out of his way to service his wife's car on Saturday, rather than taking care of his own interests. His wife doesn't notice. Or, a wife makes her husband's favorite meal, complete with an exotic dessert that takes hours to prepare. Her husband doesn't notice, gobbles it down, and rushes off to a meeting at church.

SOLUTION: Use phrases like: "Honey, you must have something on your mind. Are you okay?" Then, listen. Afterwards, say: "I knew there was something wrong because it is so unlike you not to notice I fixed your car (or fixed your favorite meal)." This is the partner's cue to say, "Oh, I'm so sorry. Please forgive me, you know I just love it when you do special things for me. I'm sorry. My mind was somewhere else. How can I make it up to you?"

PROBLEM: Your mate begins to criticize you over a long period of time and you've ignored it up until now. For example, he dislikes the food you are cooking.

SOLUTION: During a talk time say: "Honey, It really hurts when you criticize my cooking. I realize from your point of view, it's no fun coming home to unappetizing food. Can we come up with a solution? What do you suggest?" There are many possibilities that should come up in the conversation: cooking school, the husband offering to cook every other night, or helping his wife better understand what he likes.

PROBLEM: The wife criticizes her husband for neglecting the house. Maybe she expects him to paint or fix a leaking faucet.

SOLUTION: Have an honest discussion to understand the real problem. If it's a lack of skill, the husband could tell his wife that he's sorry that he isn't a handyman, and suggest they work on putting extra money in the budget for these kinds of needs.

PROBLEM: How do you forgive the mate who thinks of himself or herself first and is selfish from time to time?

SOLUTION: Address the situation in talk time. For example, "I know you didn't mean to, and it is so unlike you, but when you used our overflow money fund for a new chain saw without asking me, I felt hurt. I was thinking of using it for the two of us to go on an extended weekend trip. Next time, please tell me your plans and I'll tell you of mine. We can discuss it and even pray about it." Be ready to say, "I'm sorry. Please forgive me. I just wasn't thinking. Please forgive me for being selfish. I love you."

CHAPTER 6

SACRIFICE VERSUS SELFISHNESS

The following week, I was a speaker in a Sunday night fireside for married couples. My assignment was *Sacrifice Versus Selfishness in Marriage.* Sitting on the stand, my eyes surveyed the audience. I was looking for Jake and Sarah. Where were they? They had promised me that they'd attend to learn about secret number six. The Bishop introduced me. I walked to the podium, smiled, and began my talk.

"Mention the word sacrifice at an office party, and you will receive a lecture on the modern value of self-fulfillment. It all began in the sixties. Women not only were college educated in large numbers, they also had all the advantages of modern household inventions that eliminated the enormous amount of time and drudgery of housework. With time on their hands, they wanted fulfillment outside the home. However, the traditional values of family life were still the mainstream pattern of our society. Many of our parents fought in World War II and were, themselves, products of the depression when sacrifice was a way of life. They never questioned the value of working harder so that their children could rise above them economically. They sacrificed having new cars, boats, clothes, expensive vacations, and memberships in social clubs, in order to save enough money to put their children through college. In some cases, they sacrificed their own personal happiness in a marriage for the sake of the children.

"When the counter culture hippie movement impressed upon the youth that it was time to think of *oneself*, a drastic change occurred in our society. Marriages turned into institutions whose purpose was to satisfy the needs of the individual. If a husband or wife felt neglected, put upon, or used in any way, it was time to bail out and get a divorce. The purpose of marriage was, 'What can you do for me?' 'How can you fulfill me in the marriage?'

"The idea of service in marriage was out. The idea of sacrifice in marriage was abhorrent, and counterproductive to one's own personal development. Wives working as secretaries to put their husbands through medical school became a thing of the past. Women were now leaving the children with the husband, and venturing out into the world to *find themselves*. One famous woman who did just that was Margaret Trudeau, the wife of the Prime Minister of Canada. She left the children! She left her husband! She journeyed all over America partying and experimenting. Her antics were highly publicized.

"What happened to the word *sacrifice*? It still is one of the foundations of the gospel of The Church of Jesus Christ of Latter-Day Saints, and a part of covenants we make in the temple with the Lord. Unfortunately, many people today equate sacrifice with self-deprivation and consider it a negative behavior to serve others when it seems to interfere with our individual happiness. The modern day divorce rate reflects a general consensus in today's world, which says: 'You need not stay in a marriage if you're unhappy. Sacrifice for the sake of the well-being of the children is not necessary. One should think of one's own happiness.' We can easily see that this worldly philosophy has failed, as evidenced in the epidemic breakdown of the family in our culture.

"Sacrifice is the ultimate expression of love. In marriage, it is giving of yourself so that your mate feels loved. It is a willingness to confront problems, not simply to take the easy way out. It is understanding that this process, of working out problems with your partner, is one of the most important ways we learn to be better people. It is giving up selfish ways so that you are a better mate in your marriage. If you think of marriage as a refining process, you realize that the challenges you face are necessary. Each one is like a grinding stone polishing one more facet in your relationship. When you conquer problems, often through sacrifice, you are that much closer to a celestial marriage on earth.

"It is very common for women in their forties to go through a period called a 'mid-life crisis.' By that age, a woman usually has her children in high school or even college. She has a little more time to herself. If she was a 'stay-at-home' mom, she may look at her husband's successes and long to know what life would have been like if she, too, had a career out of the home. Assuming that she and her husband were living righteous, spiritual lives together, that they prayed about every significant family decision: when to have the children, where to live, new career opportunities, etcetera, one might think that life would be complete. However, a longing can occur, especially for a woman who achieved a considerable amount of success before she married. Changing diapers, wiping running noses, talking to children all day, supporting a husband as a bishop, caring for the sick in the ward, volunteering for the PTA, organizing quilt-making for the homeless, and doing other service projects, is an entirely different kind of fulfillment when compared to earning a raise at work, having a paper published, or performing research to find a cure for cancer.

"It is common for a woman to feel like a sacrificial lamb. I confess I began to feel this way myself. As I entered my forties, although we had always prayed about each major event in our lives and made all our decisions together, it was easy to feel that I was the servant of all. I was wishing I could have accomplished so much more in my life. I had gladly chosen to start a new business with my husband, and to support my children in their endeavors. I loved serving others at church and in the community. And yet... I had not fulfilled some of my own dreams.

"A few years ago, we decided to take a BYU tour to Israel and Egypt with our children. Each stop was a spiritual experience. When we arrived at the House of Caiaphas, where Jesus was taken immediately after his arrest in the Garden of Gethsemane, we saw a spot where, more than likely, Christ was flogged 39 times. Entering into the dark, dank, basement of the house now situated below the Cathedral of Galicantu, I was overcome with an intense emotion. I had to put on my sunglasses to hide my tears. In my previous studies, I had always concentrated on the gift of the atonement, never on the pain and agony Christ suffered. Now my attentions were focused on the physical torture he endured in order to give us the gifts of forgiveness, resurrection, and eternal life. Christ knew that it wouldn't be pleasant. He knew it wouldn't be easy. But, He had a mission to perform, and He was willing to accomplish it fully by sacrificing his mortal life without complaint. He demonstrated unconditional love. He showed us by the supreme sacrifice He made for us.

"Suddenly the thought went through my head, 'It isn't in your worldly accomplishments by which you shall be judged but by the very sacrifice which you give to others, even as Christ did. By this you shall be judged.' A wonderful feeling from the Holy Spirit filled my soul, testifying to me that this was a personal revelation from the Lord. How could I ever complain again? For the first time in my life, I felt that I knew the true meaning of sacrifice. I thought about Christ nailed to the cross and saying aloud, 'Father, forgive them for they know not what they do.' (Luke 23:34).

"When we sacrifice for others, not as a martyr, but as service, to help our spouse and children accomplish their missions on earth, we are doing the Lord's work and perfecting ourselves. We are serving a powerful mission.

"If Christ had not sacrificed his life for us, we could not fulfill our destinies. We literally needed His sacrifice to live again, and to have eternal life. Likewise, without the sacrifices we make, our spouse, children, and loved ones, cannot achieve their missions on earth.

"Think about some of the great men and women who have sacrificed their own desires to help their spouse fulfill a destiny. People who come to mind include Emma Smith, Sariah in the *Book of Mormon*, and the hundreds of women who took care of the home and family while their husbands served missions for the Lord. Their sacrifices allowed a great work to be accomplished. Without them, it would not be possible.

"There is a wonderful book by Elaine Cannon called *Minerva, the Story of an Artist with a Mission*. It tells about the sacrifice made by Herman, Minerva's husband, when she was asked to paint murals in the Manti Temple. She had to leave her home for months to accomplish a great work. Herman was left on their farm without her constant help and companionship. He gave her emotional support, testifying that her work was of the Lord and that he would do what was necessary to help her accomplish her calling. Early in their marriage, he knew that his wife had a mission as an artist. He supported her, encouraged her, and prepared the way by which she could accomplish this portion of the measure of her creation.[4]

"I saw my mother sacrifice much for our family. She told us many times that she felt guided by the Lord, early in her youth, to pursue an education, and to develop a career that would prepare her for earning a living to help her family. Her nursing profession enabled her to help my father finish his college education, and to fund ballet and music lessons for her daughters. She always supported my father in every calling he had in the church, and she never complained. My mother had many talents that she didn't have a chance to develop further. As I look back, I realize that if she had focused solely on herself and her own needs, my sister, my father, and I never would have been able to achieve our purposes on earth. She felt strongly that she was accomplishing an important mission on earth by supporting all of us. Fortunately, in the second half of her life, she was able to pursue many of the things she loved to do, including writing and gardening. We will forever be in her debt.

"It is important to note that my mother was never a martyr. She and my father were a team. They discussed, researched, and studied

---

[4] Elaine Cannon, *Minerva, the Story of an Artist with a Mission* (Bookcraft, SLC, Utah)

each decision carefully, prayed about it, and then proceeded with the knowledge that they were each doing what the Lord wanted them to do.

"Togetherness is the key to sacrifice in marriage. If a couple prays about choices, they will discover the Lord's plan for them. Then, a sacrifice of one's personal desires can actually become a joy. In fact, the word sacrifice, in this case, becomes synonymous with personal choice.

"Sacrifice is a necessity for nearly any achievement in life, whether it be learning to play the piano, becoming an accomplished singer, dancer, artist, writer, doctor, or lawyer. The list is endless. I remember walking to my ballet lessons after school, rather than playing with my friends. Sometimes I wished I could be like the other kids, free to play. Those thoughts were only fleeting, however, because my top priority then was learning how to be an exceptional dancer. Our son, Alexander, was driven to perfect his swimming skills. He sacrificed many other activities to practice swimming for three hours a day, six days a week. His sacrifice, (I prefer to call it his choice) was rewarded with a swimming scholarship to BYU. Any success we achieve in this life does not come to us without sacrifice. Sacrifice is a fundamental law of the universe. So, too, sacrifice is a necessary part of achieving a celestial marriage on earth.

"Resentments can occur in a marriage when a couple doesn't pray about a sacrifice that will be made on the part of the wife or husband. For example, when a husband is called to be a Bishop, the couple should pray about it and receive a witness that the calling truly came from the Lord. Then, it is easy for the wife and children to sacrifice all the hours of not seeing their husband and father, so that he can serve the Lord. When a husband is performing his duty as a Bishop by helping a couple learn how to budget on a Saturday, and his wife needs him to mow the lawn, it is easier for her to take over that responsibility when she knows that she is performing the Lord's work by supporting her husband.

"I think about my daughter who has waited for me many times in the car after her Young Women's meetings, until I finished counseling a couple with marital problems. Never once would she complain. She always felt that she was serving the Lord by supporting me in my church calling. I have always been grateful for her pure spirit and understanding of sacrifice.

"The other day, my sister, Betsy, reminded me of a great sacrifice one of our ancestors made. Her name was Elizabeth Dorsey. She was sailing aboard a passenger ship from Ireland to the United States, with her husband and two sons. The family was eager to immigrate in order to find a better life. Elizabeth was a doctor. During the voyage, many passengers were stricken with typhoid fever. Elisabeth spent hours caring for them. Her sacrifice was a mission to the Lord, through service to others. Unfortunately, she contracted typhoid fever herself, and died shortly before her family landed on Ellis Island. She made a supreme sacrifice for others, and her efforts are indisputably recognized as angelic."

I stopped for a moment, ostensibly to catch my breath and take a drink of water, but also to look through the audience. I still couldn't see Sarah and Jake, but the chapel lights were dimmed and a set of spots were shining in my eyes, so it was hard to tell just who was in the audience. I set the glass back down on its shelf by the podium and continued.

"The opposite of sacrifice is selfishness. As a little girl, I remember a lady in our ward who spent more than her husband earned. She was an odious woman determined to dress like a Parisian model in *haut couture* despite her 'Sears' budget. One day, her husband, out of desperation over finances, pointed a gun to his forehead and pulled the trigger. Selfishness destroyed their marriage and his life.

"The scriptures are replete with examples of selfishness. King David was a man who had everything: talent, power, favor with the Lord, and many wives. In an act of selfishness, he had another man killed so that he could possess the man's wife. When the Nephites became prosperous, they had a pattern of looking down on the poor, reviling them for their lowly state. Their selfishness became their downfall. If they had only sacrificed by sharing some of their time, knowledge and abundance with the downtrodden and helpless, they would have continued on the road to perfection.

"*Marriage is hard.* We hear this cliché all the time. We hear it from therapists, husbands and wives, and from the pulpit. 'The longer we're married, the harder it becomes,' is another common sentiment. I really take issue with this statement. It implies that our mates are tough to live with. It infers that they are the reason that marriage is hard. I believe it is just the opposite. Marriage isn't hard. What is hard is giving up our *cherished imperfections* on the altar of sacrifice to make a marriage run smoother. In other words, it's hard to change ourselves.

"What do I mean? Here is an example. My husband and I were on our annual honeymoon without the children, on the Hawaiian Island of Molokai. We entered our hotel room on the second floor. We had requested the upper level because I'm afraid of geckos. By being on the second floor I hoped the geckos would be less likely to invade our space.

"The first night, I spotted a large gecko crawling up the wall. I was horrified and screamed for help. Any normal husband would say, 'That's ridiculous. Geckos are harmless. In fact they are good. They eat bugs. There is no logical reason why you should be afraid of them. So, just ignore them.' Then, he would have ignored me and continued to relax or read a book.

"But my husband is not the ordinary man. He knows that sacrificing one's own desires for a loved one is an ultimate expression of love and essential to a happy marriage. So, my husband got up off of his bed and chased the gecko around until he was able to trap it in a jar and take it outside. He repeated this sequence at least once a day. I know that my gecko phobia is ridiculous. But that wasn't the point. My husband was willing to sacrifice his agenda of uninterrupted relaxation to satisfy my needs.

"Now, let's talk about the small sacrifices, not the dramatic ones we all face. A small sacrifice is going fishing with your husband, when you can afford only one vacation together a year, even though you don't like fishing. This act of love shows your husband just how much you love him. It demonstrates your desire to learn about and understand every part of his life. Sacrifice is spending the next year's vacation going to New York City to attend several Broadway plays, visit art museums and shop, because it's your wife's fondest desire, even though you'd rather be fishing.

"When Prince Charles and Princess Diana started having their marital problems, the newspapers emphasized their separate vacations. Charles was an avid hunter, introspective and philosophical. Princess Diana was fond of rock clubs and nightlife. I always thought that it was sad that Princess Diana didn't go on some of her husband's hunting trips to get to know and understand his soul. Apparently, another woman did, and she became his mistress. Likewise, it was a shame that Prince Charles didn't make a greater effort to share his wife's interests. When neither was willing to bend and sacrifice personal agenda, the marriage grew apart. Sacrifice is necessary in order to attain the oneness that we so desire in a celestial marriage on earth.

"Lastly, sacrifice is the ultimate way in which we perfect ourselves. If you have ever given up junk food or sweets to lose a few pounds, you know what a sacrifice it can be. You long to eat what you want to eat. But in reality, the sacrifice you make is better for your body. Sacrifice is part of the process of learning self-discipline, a necessity on the road to perfection.

"We all have faults that our mate dislikes. Believe me, it's a lot easier to be selfish and retain our annoying habits, than it is to change. However, when we strive to perfect ourselves, by sacrificing a fault that drives our mate up the wall, greater oneness and love are our rewards.

"When Conrad and I were in our early years of marriage, we didn't have money to spend on anything extra. So, we decided that we would start a tradition of giving of ourselves at Christmas. In fact, we decided to give each other a gift of changing something in our behavior that the other person didn't like. Now, we always look forward to what surprising change we will receive from the other person on Christmas Eve.

"Two years ago my husband told me that it bothered him that I couldn't keep the pigeon holes on our desk neat and orderly. Instead, they were usually stuffed with letters that I wanted to keep, school information, and articles and newspaper clippings I needed to file. So, for Christmas, I promised to keep them clean and organized for a year.

"One Christmas, Conrad promised me that he would take off his shoes when he entered the house. It was a dream come true because it cut down on my housework. Conrad knew that I despised taking the garbage out. It was in my psyche that a man should take out the garbage. But he never seemed to have time. I have to say that my all-time favorite Christmas present was the year he decided to take out the garbage for a full year. And you know what? He still does it! That's what happens when we change habits for our mate. It's wonderful because we are perfecting ourselves and bringing more joy to our marriage.

"One time when I was giving spiritual counseling to a couple, I suggested that they try this idea. Kristi, the wife immediately replied with enthusiasm, "I love that idea, John. Let's start doing that this Christmas."

"John was horrified and lamented, "And I suppose you're going to tell me what I have to give you each Christmas, what I have to change about myself."

Kristi answered him apologetically, "Gosh, honey, I'm sorry. I didn't mean to sound threatening. I'd never tell you what to change about yourself as a gift to me because that would defeat the purpose of what Laura called a true gift of love. It would have to be your idea and from your heart. Otherwise it wouldn't work... at all."

"I was proud of Kristi for seeing the true spirit of what I was talking about, and I could tell that her husband was relieved. After all, no one likes to be told what they have to do to change.

"I have held classes for couples over the age of sixty. These are couples who have been married for thirty-five years or more. You would think that by this time in life, they would have ironed out all the kinks, and perfected the art of loving each other. Not so. Many of them are living lives of quiet desperation, as Henry David Thoreau so aptly called it.

"After working with these older couples for some time, I discovered that one negative trait many of them have in common is an unwillingness to sacrifice for their partner, not in all areas, but in one or two critical ones. In some cases, they've made a habit of taking separate vacations because they are unwilling to explore their partner's world. Unfortunately, because they have refused to change for so long, the possibility of change now seems to be nil. If instead, they had developed the skill of sacrifice early, it would be second nature to give to each other now. Not only would the sacrifice be appreciated, but their love for each other would be refined, having grown strong through the test of time.

"What about the wife who is past menopause and doesn't feel like making love any more? Just because she has no desire, this doesn't mean that her husband wants to give up on sex. A woman who selfishly refuses to have sex with her husband, denies him the kind of love he still needs. Sharing physical love with her husband leads to love in return. This gesture of sacrifice can inspire a husband to learn new ways of love-making to ensure comfort and pleasure for his wife in her new post-menopausal state. In other words, in taking care of his needs, he would take care of hers, and neither would have the temptation to start to look elsewhere for love.

"It is hard to understand the woman who has refused to make love to her husband for extended periods, maybe even years, and then considers him the 'evil villain' when he has an affair. He has done something terribly wrong, but his wife has played a part in the wrongdoing. We all look for someone who will fulfill our love needs in marriage. We fall in love because we feel loved. We must continue in marriage to be aware of our spouse's love needs, sacrificing if we must, to fulfill them.

"Similarly, it is an inconsiderate husband who cares only about his own pleasure in sex and does not learn how to give pleasure to his wife during any stage of their marriage.

"What if a husband smacks his lips while eating, and it drives his wife crazy? It's likely that he wasn't taught in his home to observe rules of common etiquette. An inconsiderate husband is one who loves his bad habits more than sacrificing for the happiness of his wife. It amazes me when I see a man or woman simply balk at a suggestion to improve. He or she remains inconsiderate over some petty behavior, thereby stifling progression on the road to pure love. Think how much better it would be if the husband sacrificed his habit to make his wife happy. She would feel loved and he would benefit by improving his social acceptance in any circle. We all know how hard it is to change ourselves. What a compliment, what a demonstration of love it is to change a habit for a loved one! Men and women who sacrifice a flaw in their character, to perfect themselves for their mate's happiness, reap the benefits of gratitude, loyalty, and love. As the scripture says, 'Be ye therefore perfect even as your Father which is in Heaven is perfect.'

"Marriage is not hard. What is hard is changing ourselves, diminishing our imperfections so that we can be the 'perfect mate.' What's hard is learning how to love our mate, because in so doing, we have to change ourselves and make sacrifices. Change may seem difficult, but when compared to the long-term consequences of continuing a negative behavior that our spouse dislikes, it is actually easy. And the results are well worth the effort.

"What if we think that what we do is already perfect and that our mate is just finicky? I would say that this is an issue of pride. If your mate was taught to kneel down beside one's chair for the dinner prayer, and you don't think kneeling is necessary, for heavens sake give it up. Change for the sake of the marriage. Sacrifice for your mate. What difference does it make in the eternities of time? Habits? Imperfections? They are the same. Rid yourself of the ones that your mate dislikes and cause friction in your marriage. This is the art of sacrifice in a marriage. It brings the ultimate oneness and perfection in loving your spouse.

"Sacrifice for your marriage is not the same as being a martyr. It is giving up a behavior for a greater good, so that unity occurs in your marriage."

I ended my talk and returned to the newly upholstered blue seats on the stand. When I looked up, my eyes instantly connected with Sarah and Jake. They had come! Jake lifted his thumb of approval in the air and smiled. They had heard secret number six for achieving a successful celestial marriage.

ASSIGNMENT NUMBER SIX:

1. Each mate writes down all the sacrifices he or she has made for his or her partner including those which make them feel like a martyr.
2. Discuss these sacrifices with each other. Are any unnecessary sacrifices? Do they involve selfishness?
3. Discuss: Is there a way to change the individual sacrifices to make them more equitable?
4. Review each sacrifice. Ask the question: Is this a good sacrifice, one which must be fulfilled to accomplish our goals together? To accomplish our missions on earth? If so, commit to continue and rejoice in this opportunity. If not, discuss how you can change.
5. Discuss: Are there other areas where a sacrifice should be made?
6. Pray about any unresolved sacrifices between you, and ask the Lord to help you resolve them together, so that you might restore your oneness with the Lord.

CHAPTER 7

FINANCIAL ONENESS

The marshmallow was golden brown as I pulled it out of the fire—toasted to perfection. In contrast, when Elisabeth removed her marshmallow from the outdoor brick fireplace, it looked like a flaming shish kebab. By the time I blew out the fire, all that remained was a lump of sticky charcoal. She began to cry. Quickly, I handed her mine. Her mood changed instantly. She smiled with a look of gratitude, and along with Jake and Sarah's children, ran off to play on our swing set. I had invited their family over for a summer barbecue, a setting to make Secret Number Seven easier to discuss.

"So coach, what's the latest secret?" Jake asked.

"Financial oneness in a marriage."

"Arg," Jake remarked. "Right now, that's an area in which we're having a little bit of difficulty."

"What seems to be the problem?" my husband asked Jake. It was so good to have Conrad in on this session.

"Well, for starters, we haven't paid tithing this year. Not enough money. Things are too tight."

"Hmm. I see," Conrad uttered without condemnation.

"Let me start out the discussion tonight with a story," I offered.

"I love your stories," Sarah said, snuggling up to her husband.

"Years ago, after Conrad and I had owned our business for about five years, we were finally making enough money to meet payroll with a little left over for reinvesting in new equipment and improvements. Sometimes there was even enough money for Conrad to take out a salary. My ballet school and company were not our sole source of support anymore. However, from time to time we encountered difficult times. One Thursday morning Conrad lamented that he didn't know what he was going to do. Payroll had to be paid on Monday and we were $11,000 short. My first question was: 'Have we paid tithing? Are we current?' Conrad answered, 'Yes, of course, honey. You know I always take tithing out first thing and pay it.' 'Good, good. I knew you had,' I assured him.

"When we first started our business, we had agreed that we would always stay current on tithing, and pay it every month. Some people who own businesses only pay their tithing at the end of the year when they know how much money they actually earned, or because they want to earn interest on the money until they pay it all at once at tithing settlement. However, my father who had been a bishop twice, told me stories about couples who waited until the end of the year to pay their tithing, and then they didn't have the money! Even those with the best intentions would sometimes dip into their tithing fund to pay bills."

"Yeah, I know all about that," Jake said with a regretful tone in his voice.

"Keeping the law of tithing is a commandment that I have always considered a privilege to keep. After all, the Lord has given us everything that we have. Giving back only ten percent is a small thing.

"Back to the story of the payroll problem. After remembering what my father had told me about tithing, it suddenly occurred to me what we should do. I suggested, 'Let's pay $1100 now in tithing, in advance, to show our faith that the Lord will provide the $11,000.' Conrad was surprised at my suggestion. He thought for a minute and then responded. 'I'm not sure I feel right about that. After all, it's as if I'm saying give me, give me.' I didn't argue. I just agreed to support him in whatever he thought was right.

"The next day, we checked the mail for payments owed to us by our customers. Nothing had come. It was Friday, and payroll was due Monday. We still were $11,000 short. Our last chance was Saturday. That morning we went to the office and waited for the mail. It finally came. Nervously, we opened each envelope. Dollar by dollar, we added up all the checks and they totaled almost exactly $11,000. Conrad turned to me and said, 'You were right.' 'What are you talking about?' I asked. With a sheepish grin, Conrad told me what he had done. The day after I had suggested it, he had written out a check for $1100 in tithing and mailed it off. He had remembered that paying tithing is an exercise in faith, not begging. The result was a dramatic answer to our expression of faith in the Lord. To this day, our non-LDS chief financial officer asks us if we've paid our tithing when cash flow is slow.

"In my Patriarchal Blessing, which I received as a twelve year old, it paraphrased the scripture from Malachi 3: 10, 'If ye are faithful in thy tithes and offerings the Lord will open up the windows of heaven and pour thee out a blessing thee cannot hold.' This scripture in Malachi is for everyone. It is a promise that we will be able to provide for our families, and even abundantly if we keep the law of the tithe. This commandment is clear cut, and should be rule number one for financial oneness in a marriage."

Rule #1:
Pay Your Tithing First.

Conrad jumped into the conversation. "In achieving financial oneness, the first principle of budgeting is to *always* pay your tithing first. A couple should automatically deduct tithing from their paycheck in the same manner that an employer deducts taxes from your paycheck, before you ever receive it. Everyone knows that a person has to figure their living expenses on their income after taxes. The same is true in a celestial marriage. Figure your income as the sum you have *after* the taxes and tithing. Although I do not agree with government methods of forced taxation, I do recognize the fact that the government system of taking one's taxes out before they receive a paycheck is ingenious."

"Why?" Jake asked.

Conrad continued. "If you received your gross pay with no deductions, and had to send in tax money yourself, you would think twice before you gave back the amount asked of you. The temptation to keep all of the money would be great. First, a person would think about buying things they need, like Susie's much needed sport shoes, paying for ballet lessons for Karen, or a family vacation to Yellowstone National Park. Second, people would question how their taxes were being spent, and maybe decide to protest and not contribute at all. The government would have a whole new set of problems in collecting taxes. It was a brilliant move to have businesses do it for them, eliminating the possibility for the employee to make a choice."

"Yeah. That's how I feel," Jake commented. "It would be a good way to protest how the government spends our money."

"For people who do not yet understand the glorious blessings that can come from tithing, an approach such as automatically deducting tithing just like taxes is a wise idea. Later, a testimony of tithing will come, and a couple will tithe their income as a necessity, knowing it is like insurance for financial success in one's marriage."

"Thanks, Conrad. So now, Sarah, what do think about paying your tithing?"

"I think it is a necessity, don't you Jake?" She nudged him and he smiled. "We needed this."

"Let's move on to the next financial rule."

Rule #2:
Sacrifice for the future - take out another 10% for saving and investment.

"This money will come in handy if you or your husband lose your job or have an emergency. One time when I was giving pre-martial counseling to a young couple, they just about fainted when I told them to take out another ten percent of their money. 'What will we have left to live on?' They both moaned. I laughed and shared my 'living in a leaky basement' story with them. The fact is that the ten percent saved in the bank and invested is no different than collecting food storage for times of need. We all know someone who spends years chasing after *get-rich-quick* schemes. Most lead to failure. Financial success comes from practicing daily principles of thrift, savings, and conservative investments.

"Dr. Elisabeth Nielson Schafer, my sister, and Dr. Robert Schafer, Professors at Iowa State University, have always been great examples to me. When my sister and I were about to inherit a piece of property from our parents, I asked an investment counselor for some advice. He asked about my sister and her husband's financial situation. I told him, and he commented, 'I am so glad that I'm not a professor. I could never live on that salary.' He made five times their combined income. When I told him about how they lived, the many foreign trips they took, the Eddie Bauer clothes they wore, the house they lived in that was nicer than his, he was astonished. He inquired, 'How do they do it? They must live off of inherited money as well.' He was totally wrong. Neither my sister nor her husband had received money from inheritances. They had done it on their own by paying their tithing, saving and investing. They were a perfect example of steadily living the financial secrets of a successful marriage."

Conrad continued.

Rule #3:
Make a budget and stick to it.

"Make a list of all of the basic needs of life you must pay to subsist:
1. Rent or mortgage payment

2. Heating bill
3. Electric bill
4. Telephone bill
5. Water, sewer, garbage, etc. bills.
6. Car payment and monthly gasoline bill
7. Insurance: house or apartment, car, and health
8. Food
9. Debts

"After all of these necessities are taken care of, divide up the remaining money for the following categories:

1. Clothing
2. Entertainment
3. Vacations
4. Life insurance
5. Husband's personal allowance
6. Wife's personal allowance

"Do you have any large credit card debts?" Jake nodded. "Do you have medical bills you're still paying off?" Jake nodded again. "Student loans?" Sarah shook her head, 'no.'

"Payments on those all have to be deducted before dividing up the funds into the minor categories."

"This is so depressing," Jake uttered.

"It's only depressing because you've gotten yourself into financial problems. Once you follow these rules, especially by following a budget, you will get on a healthy financial track, and you and your wife will have financial harmony and freedom from debt."

This time, I continued.

RULE #4:
NEVER, *NEVER* GO INTO DEBT TO PURCHASE ANYTHING EXCEPT A HOUSE OR CAR.

"Personally, I don't even believe in even going into debt for a car. Often we have purchased second hand cars, a few years old, for cash. We wouldn't be where we are financially if I cared about having a new car. But, I know there are exceptions.

"The book, *The Millionaire Next Door*, written by Thomas J. Stanley and William D. Danko profiles today's self-made millionaire.[5] The description is surprising:

[5] Thomas J. Stanley, Ph.D. & William D. Danko, Ph.D., *The Millionair Next Door* (Longstreet Press, Inc., Atlanta, Georgia, 1996) pgs. 8-11

1. He might drive a second hand car, usually American made.
2. He lives off of less then 7% of his wealth, well below his income.
3. Half of the wives of these millionaires do not work outside the home. Of those who do, the number one occupation is teacher.
4. He shops at stores such as J.C. Penney.
5. He pays cash for most things.
6. He continually invests 15% to 20% of his income.
7. The wives are meticulous budgeters and planners.

"Heartache and bankruptcy follow the chronic spender. A chronic spender is one who has to have *things*, whether or not they need them and can afford them. I believe that many Americans who did not live through the depression and have never experienced poverty have this problem, unless they have been taught basic budgeting principles."

"Yeah we know," Sarah looked down at the grass.

"In the 1980's I was so impressed with the many Cambodians, Vietnamese, and Laotians who came to Seattle after the Vietnam War. Within a few years most of them were financially on their own and prospering. During that time, Conrad and I were just beginning to see rewards in our business. Even at that, we still had frugal Friday night dates. One of our favorites was to go to Westernco, a donut shop near our house. There for a $1.00 we could sit in a booth, drink water, and eat a donut or two. We used to stay for quite a while, and talk to our hearts' content.

"At first, the donut shop was owned and operated by long term U.S. residents. They hired Cambodian workers, generally all from the same family, to sweep the floor and handle menial chores. Little by little, the Cambodian family members took over more responsibilities, and began selling the donuts. Next, they were baking them. Although their English was broken and sometimes hard to understand, within a few years, they had purchased the donut shop! Wow! Conrad and I were in awe of these industrious and frugal immigrants. They knew how to live without a television, stereo, dishwasher, microwave oven, and new furniture. Often, two or three generations in a family would live together in small quarters to save money for their investments. These people didn't go into debt. They lived well below their incomes and saved the rest for the future."

"I guess we've always thought we had to have everything now," Jake commented.

"That's often times the case. You are representative of a great many people," Conrad continued.

RULE #5:
PROMISE YOUR SPOUSE NEVER TO PURCHASE ANYTHING OVER AN AGREED AMOUNT (e.g. $50) WITHOUT CONSULTING WITH ONE ANOTHER, DISCUSSING THE PROS AND CONS, AND PRAYING ABOUT THE DECISION TOGETHER.

"When Laura and I were first married, we had so little we had an agreement to never spend more than twenty-five dollars a month without consulting each other. The twenty-five dollars represented our own personal allowance. We didn't have to report to the other how we spent it.

"Couples who make large amounts of money would obviously have larger personal allowances. They grow with a couple's earning power. By adhering to this basic principle, couples can avoid heated financial arguments such as:

'How could you spend $3,000 dollars on a big screen TV without asking me? I wanted to save for my family reunion in upstate New York this summer. Now I won't be able to go, thanks to your selfishness.'

Or, 'I can't believe you bought gold earrings. We can't afford things like that. It'll take six months to recover financially. I thought we agreed to save our money.'

Or, 'You should talk! Last month you bought a new lawnmower without asking me. It made me so mad, I decided if you can act like that, then so can I.'

"And so it goes. The budget is thrown out the window, and seeds of divorce are sown. One could argue that a lawnmower is a necessity. Perhaps this is true. The problem was that this couple didn't plan and budget for that expense together.

"*Beware*: Never buy something that's on sale that you didn't plan for in your budget without consulting with your spouse. If you think that you have to have it, then make a telephone call to your spouse and ask for their opinion. Discuss it on the phone, and have a prayer over the phone, if necessary. This call will reap great dividends in the quality of your marriage, by increasing your unity through cooperative decision making.

"Here are two common financial problems that arise in marriage," Conrad added, handing them a sheet from my class and reading it aloud.

"TWO COMMON FINANCIAL PROBLEMS
THAT ARISE IN MARRIAGE:

1. A husband or wife is controlling and doesn't consult his or her spouse in financial matters. This is particularly common among men who are sole providers.

2. A husband or wife who spends more than the family makes and insists on having things beyond their collective ability to pay for them."

Jake looked sheepish, as Conrad continued.

"In the first case, a spouse fails to comprehend that it doesn't matter who earns the money. In a marriage, it belongs to both of them. Although a man may typically be the one who brings home the paycheck, the 'stay at home' wife is also earning money by performing household duties. *Vogue* magazine ran an article in February 1991 that quoted the replacement cost of a full-time wife/homemaker from calculations measured in 1981. Back then, if a man's wife died, and he had to hire someone to: clean the house, be a nanny to the children, launder the clothes, cook the meals, and chauffeur the children to school and music lessons, he would have incurred a cost of $46,000 a year. This amount was also the average salary for an educated, professional man at that time.[6] In other words, each spouse earns the household living equally by fulfilling different responsibilities. Furthermore, this means that the budgeting and spending of the income should be jointly and equally decided.

"The problem of overspending is a sure road to disaster. I can tell you several stories of couples that have ended up in financial disaster. One such case was shocking. A forty-year-old husband suddenly died in a hunting accident. He left his wife and children in financial ruin. The husband always had to have a new car, and every new toy on the market, from TV sets to computers, etc. They were always in debt and didn't have temple recommends because they were behind in paying their tithing. Now, church welfare is providing for the family. It's too bad they didn't understand the principle of delayed gratification for physical possessions."

Conrad had just finished roasting a marshmallow and popped it in his month, so I continued.

"Another couple was given a wonderful wedding gift. Their parents bought a house for them free and clear. The husband had finished college and law school, and was earning a good living in his profession. In spite

[6] Lisa Gubernick, *Housework's Dollar Value* (*Vogue* Magazine, Feb. 1991) pg. 121.

of this gift, they always had financial problems. Their money just seemed to fly out the door. I never could quite figure it out. They rarely bought new clothes. They were always wearing 'hand-me-downs.' They never seemed to progress financially, and ended up with six children living in a two-bedroom house. They were incapable of making financial decisions together. With six children and a single income, financial decisions are critical, but it doesn't mean that you have to be financially destitute. This family had financial problems due to making many small, bad decisions. They had no budget, so they could never determine what was going wrong. It doesn't matter how much you *make*, It matters how much you *spend*.

"I saw many of my friends going into debt in their first years of marriage. They had to have new couches, baby furniture, cars, state of the art stereos and TV sets, etc. In contrast, we sacrificed: where we lived (a leaky basement, but cheap), owning only one second-hand car between the two of us, and gathering free or garage sale furniture. After many years of sacrifice, we are now finally reaping the benefits of solid financial planning. Two of the couples who acquired all the physical goodies early, have since declared personal bankruptcy.

"So, do you have any questions, Jake? Sarah?"

"No. We just need to listen and learn from you."

I continued.

RULE #6
SET UP WRITTEN FINANCIAL GOALS AND DREAMS.

"One must respect each other's financial dreams and help to make them come true. We must not be selfish and think only of our own wants. When we are courting, a good look at the financial habits of our potential mate is important. One friend of mine decided not to marry a certain man, even after a long engagement. She was troubled by her decision because she thought she had no concrete reasons. After talking to her, it was clear that she had plenty. She worked in a Seattle department store and was living at home to save money. Her parents didn't charge her for rent, food or laundry usage. In short, she was able to live at home for free. In return, her parents asked her to do some chores around the house, and allowed her to save her money (minus tithing) for marriage. She did just that. One time, when she visited her fiancèe at his apartment, she was surprised that he had just purchased an expensive set of golf clubs. It seemed strange to her because he already had a set he inherited from his father that was just a few years old, and additionally, he rarely ever played golf. She was bothered by the fact that he was spending money on an item that wasn't a necessity, when she was doing everything possible to save for the marriage. Next, she visited his folks. It was an eye-opener. His father had a brand new sports car in the driveway. Inside the house she noticed that the furniture was old and worn. The mother apologized for the look of the house, and informed her that she had recovered the furniture twice over the course of their marriage. She had been very frugal. My friend wondered if her fiancèe would be the same as his father, spending lavishly on himself, ignoring his wife's desires.

"I told my friend that these were important warnings. She deserved a husband who would plan together financially, and with whom she could jointly realize their financial dreams. It wasn't about saving money by reupholstering a couch. What an admirable talent the mother had! The key was that it wasn't right for one spouse to scrimp and save while the other mate is out spending with no vision of the future. This was an important sign for my friend to recognize. Along with other significant factors, it was clear that these two were not meant for each other.

"In a goal setting session, both spouses should articulate their financial dreams. Some goals might include: owning a vacation cottage in the mountains where the family can develop more togetherness, taking a once-in-a-lifetime family trip to the Holy Lands to further develop testimonies of the Savior's life, remodeling the family house to accommodate the growing needs of the family, setting a budget each year for a honeymoon away from the children, or saving for a college education for each child.

"The intolerant spouse is the one who squelches a mate's dreams by insisting that they are impossible. These closed-minded partners fail to understand that they need to listen, not judge, and then pray about the goals for their spouse. For example, early in our marriage, I told Conrad that I really wanted to travel and have an annual honeymoon. At the time, we had just started a business and had no income. But, my husband didn't squelch my dream. He loved me and wanted me to have it. I knew that we were temporarily living on the edge. I was wise enough not to demand that my dream be realized immediately. Instead, we agreed that this would be a goal that would take some time to realize, and that we would be able to see it happen only when we started to earn more money.

RULE #7:
PRAY ABOUT FINANCIAL DECISIONS TOGETHER.

"A friend's husband decided to take early retirement. Unfortunately, he didn't consult his wife before making this decision. He failed to realize that this decision affected her greatly. She was not ready to end her career. He accused her of being selfish when she refused to tour the United States in a Winnebago when he retired, a dream he had talked about their whole marriage. He was ready to play for the rest of his life, but she wasn't. She still had many career goals to accomplish. As the years progressed, they stopped sleeping with each other and began to live separate lives. It would have been unifying if they had prayed about this decision together. If they had received a 'yes' from the Lord, that he was supposed to retire, then the wife would have known that it was meant to be. She would have known that the Lord had other plans for her that didn't involve continuing her career.

"Here's another example that illustrates how important it is to pray about financial matters. The Saunders earned a good living. The wife had always dreamed of going to Mexico to see the archeological ruins on the Yucatan Peninsula. It would be a family trip of a lifetime, full of togetherness and spiritual experiences. The trip was tentatively booked. Then the husband informed his wife that they would have to cancel the plans because he wanted to pay off the mortgage on their house. Indeed, this was a noble desire. The wife acquiesced, but with bitter feelings. What did the Saunders do wrong? First, they didn't discuss the alternatives. The husband merely dictated the agenda. Second, they didn't pray about the variables together, with open minds, knowing that with the Lord's help, they would both be winners. After all, the Lord knows the future and ultimately knows what is best for a marriage. If Mr. Saunders had approached his wife saying, 'Honey, you know we could take the money we were going to spend on our trip and use it to pay off the house. What do you think?' After the wife expressed her feelings about how important the vacation was to her, he could say, 'I see what you mean. I had no idea you thought of it in that way. Tonight during our talk time let's discuss it further. I would really like to study it out with you, make a decision, and then ask the Lord if it is right.' Then, Mrs. Saunders could say something like, 'I'm so lucky you are my husband. Thank you for being open minded. I know we will make the right decision together.' Once they received the answer, both partners would be ultimately happy with the decision, knowing that the Lord knew best."

By this time, Conrad had finished off a couple of marshmallows, and it was my turn to roast one. He continued the discussion on financial oneness.

"There are amazing benefits that occur in a marriage when a couple budgets together and prays about financial decisions as a team. Here are a few:

1. Peace of mind
2. Higher standard of living
3. Deeper understanding, deeper respect for each other, better communication skills
4. Financial oneness
5. Spiritual oneness
6. Blessings from living the law of tithing

"I bear testimony to you that I know financial oneness is an essential part of achieving a celestial marriage on earth. Understanding each other's financial goals, and working on them together is just as important as understanding each other's spiritual goals. We must have total understanding for each other. We must be generous with each other. And, we must at all times be open-minded and willing to take our financial decisions to the Lord. Just as the Lord blesses us with prosperity and abundance when we live the law of tithing, so too does the Lord bless us with indestructible oneness when we plan our finances as a team, and pray about major financial decisions together." Conrad spoke with such power and conviction that Sarah and Jake were speechless. I handed them their assignment as Conrad put out the fire. We agreed to meet the following week.

Assignment number seven:

1. Review your financial condition, listing all your assets and liabilities.
2. Make out financial goals.
3. Make out a complete budget with your spouse, utilizing the advice in this chapter.
4. Commit to following your budget.
5. Make all financial decisions together, except for your personal allowances.
6. Pray about any financial decisions that must be made.

CHAPTER 8

COMMUNICATION

The telephone rang, waking me up from a deep sleep. "Hello," I muttered, still groggy. On the other end I heard, "This is Sarah. We can't meet tonight. All our children just came down with chicken pox. Could you send us Secret Number Eight via e-mail? We just don't want to miss a week." "Sure," I said obligingly, without realizing that I would have to write out the secret." Four hours later I e-mailed fourteen pages to Sarah and Jake.

Sarah started carefully towel-drying her children after their soda bath. With all of their scratching on the red chicken pox bumps, she questioned the efficacy of this home remedy.

"It's here!" Jake yelled from his computer desk.

"What, honey? I couldn't hear you," She yelled back. "I'm in the bathroom drying off the kids." She continued muttering to herself. "Doggonnit! He knows I can't hear him when he shouts to me in another room. You'd think he could just walk up here and... "

"...tell me without shouting through the house," Jake interrupted, finishing her sentence. Sarah jumped with Jake's surprise appearance. "I'm sorry Sarah. I forgot."

"You always do this do me. You're so inconsiderate. I can't hear you when you're in another room."

"I just apologized. Why can't you accept it?"

"Because I know you'll do it again. You never change," Sarah huffed as she led the children into their bedroom. Jake shook his head and stomped off, irritated with his wife's inability to forgive him. The scene was a common pattern in their marriage.

After Sarah finished tucking in her pox-faced little ones, she reluctantly approached Jake who was taking the milk out of the refrigerator. He unscrewed the top and guzzled down several swallows straight from the carton. Sarah groaned.

Jake glanced at the intruder with a condescending glare. "What did I do this time, your highness?"

"You know how I hate it when you drink from the carton. It's unsanitary. How many times do I have to tell you? What are you, a retard or something? You never learn."

"Oh, you should talk, Miss Perfect Who Is Always Losing Things."

"When? Name one time."

"The camera in Mexico. Remember, you left it on the bus?"

"Okay, so one time I made a mistake."

"Oh that's not all. I'm just getting started."

Sarah put her hands to her ears. "I don't want to hear it. All you do is criticize me. I'm cooped up with these children. Serve, serve, serve, that's all I do. I've had it." She started to walk away, then dramatically spun around on her heels. Jake was a few feet away. "What was it you wanted to tell me anyway?"

"Laura's e-mail arrived... Secret number eight," Jake said with a sarcastic tone.

"Yeah, well what's it on this time? Because the other secrets aren't working for us right now."

"At least we agree on one thing. Follow me."

"Why?"

"Just do it. For once, just be obedient."

"Darn you. Why do you always have to control me?"

"I give up. When you're like this, in one of your irritable moods, I should pack a bag and go live with my parents. At least they're civil to each other."

"So it's my fault?"

Sarah and Jake huffed, and pivoted on their toes in opposite directions as if they were headed for opposite corners of a boxing ring.

An hour later, Jake approached Sarah tentatively with two copies of Laura's e-mail. He offered her a copy. She grabbed it resentfully. "What's this?"

"Laura's secret number eight, that you asked her to e-mail us."

"That's all we need right now," Sarah griped.

"Just read the heading."

Sarah glanced down at the white paper, and with resentment in her voice, read out loud. "Communication." She rolled her eyes, drew in a deep breath and flopped down on her bed. "If I didn't believe in a God before, I sure would now. Talk about inspiration. Is this what you were trying to tell me when you shouted to me in the bathroom?"

"Yeah."

"I'm sorry. I just got so mad at you... I just lost it."

Jake motioned to the bed. "May I join you?"

"Please," Sarah responded meekly.

"Shall we read it together, take turns reading out loud?"

"Please."

Jake slid onto the bed. As they propped up pillows to support their backs, the air seemed to clear.

Jake began reading first. "'There are a plethora of books on the market that document near-death experiences. Although each individual experience is unique, there seems to be a common thread that runs through these afterlife experiences. If they see Christ, or experience a bright light, and then hear a message, it is usually on this order and includes a question: "What did you do on earth to love other people?" In an address to the Priesthood in 1965, Prophet David O. McKay further added that the first question a husband will be asked when he reports to Christ will be, "What did you do on earth to give love to your wife? How well did you treat her? What did you do to make her happy?" A wife will be asked, "What did you do on earth to love your husband? How well did you treat him? What did you do to try to make him happy?"'

Sarah interrupted. "I sure flunked that one today."

"Me too," Jake admitted willingly. "I'm sorry, honey."

"Yeah, me too. We really need this. Go on."

"'President McKay taught us in no uncertain terms how important it is to learn how to give love to our companion. This can only be accomplished by perfecting our communication skills with each other.

"'Dr. John Gottman, a professor at the University of Washington, is one of the leading experts in the country on why marriages fail. He wrote a best seller called, *Why Marriages Succeed or Fail* in which he outlines what he calls the four horsemen of the apocalypse, the four modes of communication that, over time, erode the marriage relationship and result in divorce. They are: *Criticism, Contempt, Defensiveness,* and *Stonewalling.*[7] To this list I add the fifth horseman called, *Controlling*.

"'*Criticism* attacks your mate's character, and could include statements such as: "You always are so negative; You never clean up after yourself; You're a terrible cook; You're a lousy lover and never give

---

[7] Dr. John Gottman, *Why Marriages Succeed or Fail* (Simon & Schuster, New York 1994), pgs. 68-95

me pleasure." This kind of criticism also attacks one's personality, and one's feeling of self worth. One time I had a couple in my class who were going to be married in two weeks. When I talked about criticism, the husband raised his hand and said that it was his duty to criticize his wife to help her perfect herself. Everyone else in the class laughed.'"

Sarah interrupted Jake's reading. "That is funny, but not really. Everybody hates to be criticized. And that's what I was doing to you all morning. Trouble is, I don't like what you do sometimes. What is a person supposed to do?" Sarah posed with genuine concern.

"Shh! Let me keep reading."

"'It's one thing to state, "Honey, it bothers me when you tap your thumbs on the steering wheel. I'm sorry it bothers me. I wish it didn't, but it does. What can we do about this?" It's another to say, "That's disgusting, Tim. Quit it. You are so crude. Didn't your mother teach you anything?" In the first case, the words are a cue for the spouse to say, "Oh, I'm sorry. I didn't know it bothered you. I'll quit." Although the wife was criticizing her husband, she did it in a way that addressed his behavior, instead of attacking his personality. In the second case, the wife is clearly negatively criticizing her husband's personality and character. If she continued on this track, over the years, the love Tim felt for her would severely erode away.

"'Another aspect of criticism is timing. A complaint spoken at the moment of hurt can be healthy for a marital relationship if handled appropriately, especially because tension is released immediately. The opposite is holding everything in, but we can't do that forever. Hence, weeks, months or even years later, we let it out like opening up a gigantic bag of complaints and dumping them all at once. It's too late at that point. How can a mate possibly rectify all of his past sins against his beloved, and do it all at one time?

"'A great illustration of this bottling up of criticism is my friend's former sister-in-law. Unbeknownst to her husband, she kept a diary of every mistake, fault, or misdeed he ever performed. She wrote down dates and times and kept it under her mattress. Finally, after ten years of recording this negative behavior, she decided to get a divorce. To make her case in court for custody and financial settlement, she brought out her record. It was devastating. I have often wondered what might have happened if she had kept instead, a diary of his expressions of love and the good things he did. I bet things would have turned out differently.'"

"'Okay. Stop reading for a minute, Jake. I want to see if I get this concept.'"

"Alright. Talk."

"Well, bear with me for a minute. I want to try out what I said to you this morning again but in a different way. So don't get offended. I'm practicing," Sarah offered sweetly.

"I promise not to get offended."

"Thanks. What if I said to you something like this: 'Honey, I know you like to drink milk out of the carton. That's what you always did in your household when you were growing up. And I understand that totally. In my household, my mom was a nurse and a germ nut. I can't help feeling the way I do about it. Every time I see you drinking out of the carton, I think about the germs deposited on the opening and passing on to the rest of the family. I mean you might have a cold or something, and then we'd all get it. Now I don't want to feel this way. I don't want to get you upset about it, and take it out on you because I love you so much. And I know you love me. And I know you're not doing it on purpose to make me mad. What do you think we could do to solve this problem?"

"Hmm. That was good honey. I like how you sort of took the blame. It takes me off of the defensive. You know, I found myself actually listening because I didn't feel like you were attacking me!"

"Wow. It works. Just like the experts say. Read some more, please."

"'Gottman's second mode of communication that spells divorce is *contempt*. Actually, I think it is easier to define contempt as any of the following: sarcasm, hostile humor, mockery, sneering, rolling one's eyes, hurling insults, name calling, put downs, displaying arrogant behavior, and showing little or no respect. All of these forms of communication are very hurtful.'"

"How depressing. I did that one to you this morning too, when I called you a retard and said that you never learn," Sarah admitted, shaking her head.

"Don't beat yourself up. I've done the same thing to you. You know what?"

"What?" Sarah answered.

"I don't think that we would use name calling or sarcasm if we always communicated the way you just did."

"This is great. I'm excited. Read some more please."

"'Gottman's third horseman of the apocalypse is *defensiveness*. Recently, I was counseling a couple, and the husband kept saying things like: "When did I say that? Name one time." Or, he would offer excuses for nearly everything. It was as if he could never be wrong, or say: "'I'm sorry." Humility is the opposite of defensiveness. Another version of this defensive characteristic is not to acknowledge or respond to a mate's complaint, but instead to attack back with one of their many faults.

"'One time, I was driving my husband home from the airport. This was unusual because he always drives when we are together. This particular day he was exhausted from a grueling week in Los Angeles, so he asked me to drive home. As soon as I merged into heavy traffic, he started to criticize my driving. Instead of me saying, "Oh, I'm sorry, honey. Do you think you can bear with me? Or would you prefer to drive? Would driving us home make you more comfortable?" I became defensive. I said, "As if you've never done the same thing? Your driving is far from perfect." That started an avalanche of negative conversation between us. He responded, "Name one time. I've never driven that way. Go on. Name one." I retorted, "I don't remember. Unlike you, I never criticize the many little driving mistakes you make. I overlook your faults."

"'This conversation is laughable now. Defensiveness like that accomplishes nothing. It just drives a wedge between husband and wife. It is far easier to just say, 'I'm sorry.' In some situations, this is sufficient and the damage is repaired quickly. Where two people are constantly using defensiveness, it may take a lot more work to change direction. In the driving situation, if only I had replied sweetly, "'I'm so sorry my driving is bothering you. Would you prefer that I pull over so that you can drive us home?" Knowing my husband, he would have then replied, "No, that's okay. I'm just on edge from my exhausting schedule. Please forgive me for criticizing you." By responding in a positive way to the criticism, I would have defused the situation before it got out of hand. That would have been the end of the confrontation. Both of us would have felt understood and loved. Instead, my defensive response destroyed an hour of what should have been a loving time together driving home.

"'Even though my husband was at fault for criticizing me in the first place, the real issue was learning to control my response, and ending the conflict before it began by answering in a loving way. After all, I could forgive his outburst. He didn't really mean it. He was tired and simply needed a good night's sleep. I've found that avoiding defensiveness also has a side benefit. Over the long term, his desire to strike out at me when he's tired has diminished considerably.

"'If we stop and think, before we answer an attack with defensive remarks, we have a better chance of understanding the real issues. If we pause, knowing full well that our mate truly loves us and wouldn't want to do anything purposefully to hurt us, we will be miles ahead in creating unity in our celestial marriage.'"

"I never really understood what I was doing. This information is invaluable," Sarah added.

"'Gottman's fourth horseman is *stonewalling*, or refusal to talk about a problem. We've all seen the movies in which the main character walks away from conflict, rather than stay with his girlfriend to discuss the issue at hand. This frustrates the audience. They want him to work it out with her. In a movie, this is a dramatic device the writer uses to create tension. In real life, it's a tragedy.

"'Some stonewallers claim that they are waiting to cool down to get their temper under control. It is often good to have a cooling off period after a disagreement, and prearrange for a discussion later. However, real stonewallers are conveniently unavailable or blatantly refuse to confront a problem now or in the future. They want to bottle it up, with the misguided hope that it will "just go away." Often stonewallers have been burned, and have developed the habit of stonewalling from a reaction to something that has caused them pain.

"'Remember going to school and having a teacher claim, "If you ever have any questions, just ask. I really want you to be comfortable in asking questions. No question is stupid. I want you to learn and thrive in my class." Soon after hearing this "open discussion" policy, a student raises his hand and asks a question. The teacher responds, "You weren't listening. I already answered that question days ago. If you had been paying attention, you would know the answer." The student was punished verbally for asking a question, exactly what the teacher had promised not to do. In this instance, the teacher taught the student to stonewall the question. He may never ask a question again, wishing not to be humiliated in front of the class.

"'In a marriage, the same thing can happen. If we're not aware of this process, we may actually train our spouse to be a stonewaller. If we punish our mate for trying to discuss an issue, we will train him or her to stop discussing. If we don't listen, or if we criticize how our mate expresses a thought, we will train him or her to stop talking. People avoid that which is painful. On the other hand, if our partner comes into the marriage with the habit of stonewalling, we must foster and encourage open discussion by creating a *punishment free zone*. We must help our mate know that they can talk about their thoughts, feelings, and beliefs without any negative judgement from us. Stonewalling is a difficult communication pattern to change. However, by giving a mate unconditional love, over an extended period of time, they will learn to trust, knowing he or she is truly living in a judgement free marriage.

"'My additional fifth horseman of communication breakdowns is *controlling*.'"

"Yeah, Jake," Sarah chided her husband. "Case in point. A half hour ago when you demanded that I follow you to see Laura's fax, and I asked why, you went into your controlling mode, telling me to be obedient."

"Okay. Guilty as charged," Jake admitted with humility. "I don't know why I do that. I guess it's because you are so strong-willed."

"It takes one to know one," Sarah teased back.

"You got me. Let's read on."

Sarah pinched her thumb and forefinger together and passed them across her pressed lips, indicating a zipping motion.

"Thank you. Now stay zipped up until I finish this," Jake responded. Sarah began to laugh, then recovered her composure to listen.

"'Some Mormon men think, because they have the Priesthood, they have the right to boss their wife around. But this is unrighteous dominion. Prophet Gordon B. Hinckley made it crystal clear in the 1997 revelation from the Lord called *Proclamation on the Family*, that men and women are equal partners in a marriage. The power of the priesthood is the power to serve others, even when it is administrative in nature. Some men use it as an excuse to justify their perceived need to always be in control. They are more comfortable giving orders to their wife than listening to her. This kind of behavior is a throwback to the immaturity of childhood when they perceived themselves as the center of the universe, and that everything around them was created for their use. Women can also be guilty of this controlling behavior.

"'Controlling communication patterns come in several packages. One is the struggle between two people for control in making decisions. When my husband and I were on our honeymoon, we drove through France. It was a dream come true for me. I was back in my mission field. What memories! We visited one member, who was married to the French artist, George Blanchard. She was surprised to see me and invited us into her modest apartment where the walls were lined with her deceased husband's paintings. She introduced me to her non-member friends visiting her from Cannes, and I introduced my husband. I explained temple marriage to them. They were fascinated. Then Madame Blanchard asked me to sing for her guests. I sang a few selections from *My Fair Lady* and we said our good-byes. As we left, I heard her answering questions about the church.

"'That visit brought back all the memories of my mission. I felt like I was home. I guess it also made me feel that I was in control of the rest of our French travels. So, I took control. Everything was fine, until one day when we went into a large store called *Carrefort*. Since I spoke almost fluent French then, I felt like the leader. Conrad, a leader himself, was surprised by the way I took control. After all, he had taken French in college and understood the French people perfectly well. As we entered the store, we each pulled in a different direction. He wanted to see one thing and I wanted to do another. I expected him to follow. He was taken aback by his new bride who turned out to be such a strong leader. I remember that we ended up in lively discussion, probably better named an argument. We were both vying for the leadership of our newly formed marriage. After a few minutes of disagreement over things that were quite inconsequential, we both had the same revelation. We had two choices: get an annulment or learn how to communicate without trying to control each other. Within a few minutes, we decided that, in any given situation, we would predetermine who would lead, and the other one would have to follow. For example: In Italy we decided that Conrad would lead and determine where we would go and how we would get there. He had visited Italy extensively and clearly had experience. It was easy to say, "Of course dear. Whatever you'd like." After all, I had never been there, and was excited for any opportunity. In France, he agreed to follow my lead. It wasn't always that cut and dried, but generally we learned that in small things, it was better to pick a leader than to pick a fight.

"'Little did we know how important this practice would be in our marriage. As the years rolled by, we found that we were always in agreement over the important matters of life such as: goals, living gospel principles, serving others, financial matters, our business, solving problems, and making important decisions about our future using the prayer method. But, when it came to the unimportant and mundane, we could almost guarantee that we would disagree. For example when I had a ballet company, and toured it around the greater Seattle area, sometimes we had to set up chairs for the audience. Speedily, Conrad and I would dive into the job. He would start setting up the chairs one way, and I would start setting them up another. Rather than argue about whose way was best, we would simply decide whose territory it was. Once determined, the other would follow. I loved it when he was on my territory, ballet. That meant he had to follow my ways, my procedures. When we were on a set filming a show, Conrad was and still is the director and boss. I follow his lead even if I think my way is more efficient. I laugh as I say this, because Conrad and I love to tease each other about efficiency, even though we willingly follow each other with wholehearted support.

"'A second form of controlling behavior in communications is more subtle, yet potentially more devastating.'"

"Brace yourself, Jake. Let's hope this isn't us too!" Sarah gulped, then nudged him to read on.

"'Conrad had been commuting to Los Angeles for six months. He would work in Seattle on Monday, fly to LA on the 6:30 a.m. flight Tuesday morning, work on his documentaries there for three days, return home at 7:00 p.m. Thursday night, sometimes drive straight to the Stake Center for meetings, and then work in the Seattle office on Friday and Saturday. Sunday morning he would begin his first church meeting at 6:00 a.m. Needless to say, he was busy. One day, after a particularly difficult week dealing with people in LA, Conrad was discouraged. When I entered his office, he looked troubled, and he complained of numbness in two fingers of his left hand. He felt that perhaps he was starting to have a heart attack. He wanted to go to the doctor. I suggested he have a blessing from David, a Priesthood holder, our production manager on the documentaries and right hand man in the business. Conrad agreed. David was inspired to tell him that the pain would subside and go away, and that he would be fine. He told him that this would not get in the way of the work he had to accomplish.

"'After the blessing, I knew that Conrad was okay. He was now under God's power of healing influence. I didn't feel that Conrad needed to go to the doctor. But, rather than tell him he shouldn't go, or trying to control him, I remained quiet and listened to his needs. He wanted to go to the doctor, and wanted me to go with him. At that moment, that was the last thing I wanted to do. I had meetings with two of my managers, a magazine article I had to finish writing by the end of the day, e-mails and correspondence to answer, and an employee problem to solve. Inside my heart, I knew a visit to the doctor's office was unnecessary. I was positive the doctor would tell him he was fine, just as the Lord had promised in the blessing. However, if I turned on the communication pattern of trying to control his behavior, it would drive a wedge in our marriage, and show a lack of love and understanding to the person I cared most about in the world. I took a deep breath, and mentally resolved to give him the kind of love that he needed. The incident turned out as I had predicted. The electrocardiogram was normal, and the doctor told Conrad the numbness was probably caused by a pinched nerve.'"

"I bet she was wishing she had stayed at work. It was a waste of time going to the doctor," Sarah puffed.

"Shh! Listen" Jake continued reading.

"'I could have resented all the time I lost at work, thinking it was a waste going to the doctor with Conrad. And that is how controllers think. They see their perception of any situation as the only correct one. Seeking to understand someone else's needs, especially if they appear to be imaginary, is not in their repertoire of behavior. They think that their view is always right. And, they think it's their privilege and duty to control others because they believe they know what is best."

"Yeah, that's how I feel so often with you, Sarah," Jake added. "I know things that you don't. Things that could save us a lot of time if you would just listen to me."

Sarah frowned. "Finish the story."

"'My husband needed to go to the doctor for his own peace of mind. I didn't need to go because I knew he was okay by the Spirit of the Holy Ghost and the blessing. But Conrad was the one who counted in this incident. Driving back to the office from the doctor, Conrad admitted that he was so relieved. He admitted that his stress and anxiety levels were so high that he barely heard the blessing. In short, he was panicked. By investing in my husband, by giving him the kind of love that he needed, by taking him to the doctor, I showed him how much I loved him. He was grateful at a very deep emotional level. His love for me increased. A day later we discussed the importance of that incident during our talk time. For Conrad, two important events happened. First, his testimony grew even deeper about priesthood blessings. He was reminded of the power of healing even when a person doesn't hear or understand a blessing. Secondly, he felt deep unconditional love from his wife, who was sensitive and willing to sacrifice her needs for his.'"

"That's a heavy concept," Sarah sighed. Jake nodded in agreement and read on.

"'A woman I'll call Judith, formed a children's choir. She was so successful with the children that she was able to tour them all over the state of Washington and even Europe. In England, she met a school choir director who was very impressed with her students. Together they started an exchange program. She continued her work successfully for ten years. Then her husband received a transfer with his job to New York City. They prayed to know if this was the right move for them. They both felt good about the decision to move. She dissolved her choir and moved. That summer the English choir director came to New York City on holiday. She telephoned Judith to meet her for lunch. Judith's husband refused to let Judith go. "What do you want to do that for? It's a waste of your time. You aren't in that field anymore. You know we agreed not to let people take up our time who don't matter to us anymore. I can't let you go. You'll thank me later." His words were intimidating and controlling. She felt she had to say "no" and cut off her friendship with the English choir director.'"

"They should have prayed about it," Jake interjected.

"That's great you thought of that, Jake?" Sarah said on a note of astonishment. "Why don't you think of that for us?"

"Gulp," Jake swallowed. "In self-defense, I have to say I've never controlled you on an issue like that."

"Uh huh. I bet that's what all controllers say. It's hard to see your own mistakes." Sarah lamented.

"Have I really been that bad?" Jake asked sincerely.

Sarah nodded her head.

Jake apologized. "Gosh, I'm truly sorry. Forgive me?"

Sarah leaned over to kiss Jake.

"Shall I take that as a yes?"

"Uh-huh."

"Good, I'll read more."

"'I have counseled several controllers. They are the kind of people who slide their index finger in a slashing motion across their throat like a cutting motion if they think their spouse has been on the phone too long. They are the kind of person who won't let their spouse go to a family funeral because it would be a waste of money. They refuse to pray about issues before making a decision. They are closed-minded about almost anything their spouse wants. They say things like, "Why on earth would you want to do that? You don't want that kind of a vacuum cleaner. We're going to get this one. You don't want to live in the suburbs near your friends. You want to live in the city like me. I'm not going to let you go to that overnight Relief Society meeting because you have better things to do."

"'Unfortunately, many marriages have failed because a husband or wife acted like a controller in important decisions. They know what is best, they say, and refuse to discuss, study or pray with their spouse about critical issues. They are little Hitlers, dictators in the family. They control by bullying, manipulating, verbally threatening, and sometimes physically abusing their victim until he or she becomes compliant.

"'I have identified three solutions to eliminate this controlling communication pattern. *First*, determine who is the leader for each unimportant situation of life where petty arguments might occur. *Second*, allow your spouse to do what they need for their personality, rather than yours. This will pay immeasurable dividends, especially in increased understanding for you when the tables are turned. *Third*, pray about decisions together rather than dictating what should be done. This creates the oneness you both desire.

"'All communication breakdowns have two sides. A willingness to examine both is required to break through problems that have developed in a marriage. It takes courage and humility to change behavior cycles. It helps to have two people working together. That's the wonderful power of a good marriage.

"'I like to think of a marriage as a business partnership.'"

"That's strange. What on earth does she mean by that?" Sarah queried.

Jake continued. "'The husband and wife are the owners of the business. And the business is marriage. We can liken it to a store. Naturally the owners, the partners, want the store to be a booming success. In order to accomplish this, the business partners must be in harmony with one another, make all business decisions together, and work long hours to succeed. The business will succeed or fail in direct correlation to the working relationship of the partners. Marriage is the same. It is a separate entity from the two individuals, and succeeds only if the partners are harmonious, make all of their major decisions together, and spend long hours to make it work.'"

Sarah interrupted. "I like the idea of separating the marriage from the individual partners. Then when things go wrong, we can examine our business, the marriage, without attacking the partners."

Jake commented. "Yeah. We can ask ourselves how to make our business more profitable, how to make our marriage more successful. Earlier today, our business, or marriage, was operating in the red. We were hurting each other. Now it's in the black, and we're happy. Right?"

"Agreed, honey. I feel relieved that we're learning how to communicate to solve our problems. From now on, we just have to ask ourselves, 'How can we solve these problems to have our marriage successful again? To feel love from each other again.'"

"That's great, Sarah. Okay, I'm going to read more now."

"'Since criticism in marriage is so destructive, it's much better to find other ways to communicate displeasure with your spouse. You can avoid the sting of criticism by addressing your concerns, not for how something hurt you, but more for how it affects the marriage. For example, suppose you said something like this at a dinner party: "Don't ask my wife to bring food to the church dinner. You won't recognize it. The only thing she knows how to do is dial Chinese-take-out." You might have thought it was funny, but your wife was deeply injured by your careless remark. She could just let you have it, and criticize you back for being so insensitive. It might make her feel good for a few minutes, but the long-term effect would be harmful to your marriage. Instead, she could say something like: "Honey, that comment you made at the dinner party really hurts us. I know you didn't mean to hurt me but when you do that, it really hurts our marriage. It makes us look bad as a couple and creates bad feelings between us." By addressing the concerns about the marriage, you accomplish what you want, calling attention to the event so it won't happen again, but you avoid the harm of attacking each other.

"'When your spouse says something that you don't like or says something hurtful, make no value judgements. Simply state that what they have said or done affects the marriage negatively. Then state how it makes you feel. For example, if a husband has the habit of spreading the daily newspaper all over the living room, the wife should not say, "You are such a slob. You are so messy. You never clean up after yourself." This only causes resentment and may trigger defensive behavior. Instead, she should say, "Honey, when you don't pick up the paper and put it away, it hurts our relationship because it makes me feel resentful that I have to pick up after you. I love you so much and our relationship means more to me than anything in the whole world. What can we do so that this doesn't hurt our marriage?" This gives the other person a challenge to help solve the problem with you. By using 'I' statements, phrases which express how something makes you feel, you will direct the discussion into a problem solving mode instead of a conflict and ego stand off. This method also allows the offending individual a chance to apologize without losing face.'"

"I get it," Sarah exclaimed. "This stops an argument before it has a chance to begin. After all, we do love each other. We just haven't acted like it sometimes."

"You're right. Let's try it. Just remember though, I might forget. Habits are hard to break. Be easy on me."

"That goes for me too. How about we have a special phrase between us to get us back on the path if we forget that we should be talking about our marriage? How about: 'Let's rewind and try that again?'"

"Good. I like that. That will remind us to think about what we've learned and actually use it."

"It'll give us a chance to redeem ourselves."

"All right!" Sarah and Jake slapped their hands together in a "high five" sign.

Jake started to read again. "'My husband frequently teases me when we use this technique. After I tell him about something that he has said or done that hurts our marriage, I will tell him what I want to hear from him right then. He laughs and then says that he is terribly sorry, thanks me for writing the script for his new lines, and as sincere as he can be, he says the words I want to hear. And now, he has learned to do the same for me. This may sound corny to some, but for us, this kind of response puts millions of points in our love bank. By doing this, we use marital problems as a way to come closer together, instead of allowing them to separate us.

"'Growing up in my family, we had a habit of always saying "I love you" as the last expression uttered in almost every conversation. I'll never forget when we visited my parents for dinner on Easter Sunday in 1989. When it was time to go home, we hugged and said the usual heartfelt "I love you" as we left the house. The next day I got a phone call. The man on the phone said that my father had passed away while working on his apartment building. I was in shock. How grateful I was that my very last memory of my father was our exchanging the words "I love you."

"'In his book, *Why Marriages Succeed or Fail*, Dr. Gottman says that every marriage has a special imaginary bank account, with love as the currency of exchange. In this account, love can be deposited and withdrawn. When we give love to our partner, we create a deposit. When we do something that hurts them, we are taking a withdrawal. Gottman says that it's a proven fact that when you have too many withdrawals of love from the account, and not enough deposits to compensate, a marriage will fail. Because withdrawals are so harmful, they must be balanced with even more love. The recommendation is that for every withdrawal we make, five deposits of love need to be given. In other words, in the bank account of love, we need to make five genuine expressions of love for every hurt that we cause. Of course, this is only enough to keep the account balanced. What we really need is an abundance of deposits of love so that withdrawals have little effect.'"[8]

"I know what he means. I've felt depleted many times. Jake, I feel like I give and give, and then if you do something I don't like, I fly off the handle. It's because I'm just love-starved."

"No wonder you explode sometimes over little things. Is it like an accumulation of hurt with nothing to compensate?"

"That's right, Jake. I don't mean to get so mad. It's just that it all adds up, and then I can't hold it in anymore. Thanks for understanding."

"I'll have to work on that," Jake committed sincerely and then continued reading.

"When I was a missionary, I learned that, regardless of how much love I gave to my companion, if I criticized her just once, it seemed to undo everything good that I had done. That taught me never to criticize

---

[8] Dr. John Gottman, *Why Marriages Succeed or Fail* (Simon & Schuster, New York 1994), pg. 57

my companions. After all, I wasn't going to spend the rest of my life with them. By avoiding criticism, it made for a much more pleasant mission, and placed our emphasis on service, instead of each other. A marriage is different. We are building something for eternity, but even here, there is no place for uninvited criticism. If you do fall to the temptation of criticizing your mate, remember that it will require an enormous amount of love to compensate. If you remind yourself of this principle often, you will think twice before letting out a critical comment.

"'The behaviors of love we are commanded to practice in our marriage are clearly defined in the scriptures in I Corinthians, chapter 13. We are to treat our spouse with kindness, understanding, patience unfailing, and unconditional love. All these qualities are fruits of the spirit when we are in tune with the Lord and living righteously.

"'Part of becoming one with your spouse and developing a true celestial marriage on earth is learning to communicate in a loving manner, always respecting your loved one's opinions and feelings. It is putting yourself in their shoes, and making them feel understood, appreciated and highly valued. There is truly an art to mastering communication skills so that you can achieve a celestial marriage on earth.'"

"That's the end of the reading," Jake said with a sigh. "Honey, I know I can do better."

"Me too. We've learned a lot today."

"She has some more here. You know, assignments." Jake looks over the last several pages. "Yikes! There are six exercises to do. Good thing the kids have chicken pox and we're house-bound."

Sarah laughed. "Hmm. The Lord works in mysterious ways, His wonders to perform."

Jake and Sarah hug each other. "I love you so much," Jake added.

"I love you too."

ASSIGNMENT NUMBER EIGHT:

Review the following, and discuss how these actions could harm your marriage:

COMMUNICATION FAILURE WARNING SIGNS :

1. One spouse puts the other down in public.
2. One spouse uses the other one as the butt of jokes.
3. A husband or wife calls their mate derogatory names.
4. One spouse constantly criticizes the other one.
5. One spouse stops listening to the other one.
6. A husband or wife makes excuses to be away from home as often as possible to avoid confronting problems.
7. Either spouse stops showing the other common courtesies of life such as tolerance for faults, and demonstrating interest in their spouse's daily life. Instead, they emphasize personal differences.
8. A couple can't talk or discuss anything without getting into a heated argument.
9. A couple decides to have separate bedrooms and has little or no real communication.
10. A spouse counsels with his or her parents to make decisions rather than his or her mate.
11. A husband or wife makes major decisions alone, without consulting the other.
12. A couple spends most of their free time with other couples, at church, in sports, or other activities. Dating ceases and the couple is rarely alone together.
13. A spouse continually criticizes himself or herself in front of their mate, and the mate agrees with the criticism. Added to this, making matters worse, is joking about a spouse's inadequacies.
14. A couple lets their children become more important than their marriage relationship. A spouse sides with a child against their mate.
15. A spouse criticizes their mate in front of their children.
16. A spouse confides with one or more of the children about a problem in the marriage.
17. A husband or wife always goes to a friend or someone else to seek solutions to marriage problems.
18. A couple holds grudges against each other and can't forgive and forget.
19. One mate controls the other like a little Hitler.

Review and memorize the following:

COMMUNICATION RULES FOR SPOUSES:

1. Never criticize your mate. *Never!* Learn other ways to discuss things that bother you.
2. Tell your mate every day that you love her or him.
3. Never be defensive if your mate inadvertently criticizes you. Simply say you're sorry and move on. Do not criticize in return even if it is justified.
4. Never stonewall.
5. Have daily talk time, showing empathy, encouragement, and unconditional love for your mate's feelings, ideas, and dreams.
6. Eliminate sarcasm and contempt from your communications. Analyze yourself. Are you showing contempt because you aren't getting enough respect yourself? Is your self-esteem so low that you have to be sarcastic to others?
7. Learn to edit your thoughts. Bite your tongue and think before you speak. Then, only let positive statements come out of your mouth.
8. Use "I statements" rather than blaming your mate. For example, if you start an argument, stop and say something like: "I feel grouchy right now. I'm not totally in control of myself right now." If your mate criticizes you, say something like: "I know you love me. But, right now I feel hurt by your words."
9. Always assume the best about your mate. Don't judge imagined intentions.
10. Delay talking about a problem when you are steaming with anger. Instead, set an appointed time to talk about it later, after you have cooled down.

Practice a problem solving session together:

HOW TO STRUCTURE A PROBLEM SOLVING SESSION WITH YOUR MATE

1. Start the discussion with a prayer asking the Lord to be with you and inspire you to understand each other's point of view.
2. Give each partner a chance to be heard uninterrupted.
3. Be humble and open.
4. Offer sincere empathy for your mate's feelings.
5. Write down possible solutions from each partner's point of view.
6. Come to a decision how to solve the problem.
7. Pray about the decision to know if it's right.
8. Follow your feelings from the Spirit
9. Reaffirm your feelings of love for your spouse.
10. End with a prayer acknowledging the Lord as the third partner in your marriage.

COMMUNICATION EXERCISE #1

Time: You need thirty minutes for this assignment.

When: Date Night: This is an ideal time to accomplish this assignment.

Where: At home with everyone out of the house except yourselves, or in a park or some other out-of-the-way place on a sunny day.

What: Start with a prayer asking Father in Heaven to be with you during this assignment. Sit so that you are facing each other. Do the following, in order:

1. **Wife:** Tell your husband all of the wonderful things that you love about him. Tell him what you like about his spiritual side, intellectual side, secular side, his personality, his gifts or talents, and his hobbies. Tell him the things that he does that you particularly like or admire in him. You have fifteen minutes to talk. The husband is to take notes, writing down the compliments.

Rule: The husband is not allowed to talk during this time at all. He must stay silent, soaking in the compliments. He can smile and give loving looks, but no talking.

2. **Husband:** For the next fifteen minutes the husband should repeat the same format by complimenting his wife's personality, intellect,

talents, activities, etc. She, in turn, must take notes on the compliments. (Same rule on silence)

Note: Each person may tell stories that illustrate a quality they love in their mate. Use memories. For example: "I'll never forget the time that I ran our car into the side of the house. I felt terrible. Rather than you getting mad at me and yelling at me for the stupid mistake I made, you took me into your arms and said that everything would be all right. You were just glad that I was okay. You have always been understanding in our marriage. This is one of the greatest qualities that I love about you."

Completion: Share your feelings.

COMMUNICATION EXERCISE #2

Work on improving your marriage. Think of it as a business.

Find another time you can be alone together similar to exercise #1.

1. The wife tells her husband what actions he has done that affect the "business," the marriage, in a negative way. At no time is the wife to make a value judgement on the action or to criticize the husband. *Example*: "Honey, when you forget to take the garbage out on Wednesdays, it hurts our marriage. I don't mean to feel this way, but I remember that you said you would take on the garbage as your responsibility. I get upset because I end up doing your job. This hurts our marriage relationship.

2. During this time, the husband must take notes. He is not allowed to speak. He must listen with an open heart and an open mind, being humble and teachable.

3. When the wife is finished, the husband should go through the list of actions that the wife has claimed hurt the marriage. He should respond by offering to fix each one the best he can, and ask for forgiveness from the wife. *Example*: "Wow! I am so sorry. I never want to hurt our marriage or you in any way. Please forgive me. I will make it my goal to get that garbage out each week so that you don't have to do it. I don't mind if you give me a gentle reminder. I will respond in a positive way and act as soon as humanly possible."

4. Then the wife responds right away, confirming her forgiveness, expressing her gratitude, and offering any cooperation to help her husband make the change.

5. Now turn the tables and have the husband relate problems that he sees the wife creating which hurt the marriage. Follow steps one through four.

6. After completing the exercise, the couple should compare notes and talk about their resolutions to better their relationship. They should exchange tokens of romantic love, kisses and hugs. They should verbalize to each other how much they love each other and commit to each other that they will improve their marriage, in order to work towards achieving a celestial marriage on earth. Close with a couple's prayer. During the prayer, the couple should hold hands and imagine they are in the presence of the Lord. End the date with a dinner out, picnic lunch in the park, or a walk around the block.

COMMUNICATION EXERCISE #3

Learn to use expressions of love by completing this exercise together on another date night.

1. **Wife:** Tell your husband what he does that makes you feel loved: actions, deeds, physical love, verbal love, etc.
    Examples: "When you notice what I'm wearing and tell me that I look beautiful, I feel wonderful. I feel loved when you go out of your way to fix me breakfast in bed, or my favorite meal. I feel loved when you spontaneously do something with or for me. It makes me feel like I am your number one priority in life. I feel loved when you tell me each day that you really love me and feel lucky to be married to me.
2. Husband must just listen and take notes.
3. **Husband:** tell your wife what she does to make you feel loved: actions, deeds, physical love, verbal love, etc.
4. Wife must stay silent and take notes.
5. **Wife:** Tell your husband what you do for him, from your point of view, which shows that you love him. *Examples:* "When I give you compliments, I am showing you that I love you. When I have a headache and don't really feel well, but I go ahead and make love anyway, I am showing that I really love you.
6. Husband takes notes on what his wife does to show her love.
7. **Husband:** Tell your wife what you do to show your love for her. *Examples:* "When I give you extra money in the grocery account so that you can spend it on anything you want, I am showing you that I really love you. When we have a difference of opinion and I tell you that we'll go ahead and do it your way, I am showing you that I really love you."

8. Wife takes notes and remains silent.
9. Discuss with each other how you can accept the kind of love your mate shows you. Take turns. *Example:* "All those times you cooked my favorite meal and I never said anything, well, I'm going to do better and tell you how much I appreciate it on the spot. I will recognize this expression of your love for me and let you know it."
10. Discuss: Do you both attach the same meaning to each other's expressions of love? If not, why? Talk about these differences and try to understand each other's reasons. Talk about your different backgrounds and relationships in your families to help you explain your differences.
11. Both partners write down the ways they would like their spouse to give them the kind of love they need.
12. Exchange lists and discuss each item to understand what the other spouse wants.
13. Each spouse commits to at least one new way of showing love to their spouse, using their partner's list.
14. Review the list monthly and continue to practice showing love in ways that please your spouse.
15. End with prayer. Commit to showing your spouse the kind of love he or she wants and needs. Kiss and hug. Take a walk, go to dinner or have a picnic to end on a fun note.

COMMUNICATION EXERCISE #4

Celebrate your differences by performing the following exercise.
1. Start with a prayer.
2. Each spouse should make a list on a piece of paper of the differences they see in each other that are positive and that help the marriage.
3. Compare lists and enjoy the differences that are positive.
4. Each one should now make a list of the differences in personalities that sometimes cause friction and problems.
5. Compare notes without criticizing each other.
6. Together, write a list of what each of you can do personally to improve those differences, in order to get along better with each other.
7. Resolve to make the appropriate changes.
8. End with a prayer, asking the Lord to be with you to implement these new ideas into your marriage.

COMMUNICATION EXERCISE #5

This exercise is to be written out separately by each mate and then discussed, topic by topic. Remember the purpose of this exercise is to strengthen your marriage – not hurt your spouse.

1. Something that I have been wanting to talk to you about but never have is:

2. If I could have my wish come true, this is how I would envision our relationship in ten years:

3. The problem that occurs frequently in our relationship and keeps us from achieving true oneness in communication with each other is:

4. This is how I think we should solve that problem:

5. Write down what you personally promise to do in your marriage to improve your communications with your spouse.

COMMUNICATION EXERCISE #6

1. Write down the names of several couples who have a good marriage and several who have a bad marriage.

2. Write under each "good marriage," examples of why the couples have a good marriage.

3. Write under each "bad marriage," examples of why you think their marriage suffers.

4. Share the names and examples with each other and enjoy a discussion.

5. Talk about your marriage and compare what you do right and what you do wrong to the list you made of the example couples. Now make a list of what you can do together to improve your relationship.

6. Talk about your ability to solve problems. Discuss the good things you have done and what you can do to improve.

7. Celebrate your successes.

8. End with expressions of love for one another.

Chapter 9

Romance

T wo weeks passed before I was invited to set foot inside the red brick Tudor house.

"We should have offered to come to your house," Sarah lamented.

"She has cabin-fever. I'm glad the chicken pox are gone," Jake laughed.

"Tonight's secret to a successful celestial marriage is *Romance*."

"We could sure use some of that right now. Take it away professor."

Jake and Sarah settled back on the burgundy leather couch. Jake slipped his arm across Sarah's shoulders and squeezed gently.

I began. "There is nothing more flattering than meeting an attractive person of the opposite sex who sends visual signs that they are interested in you. It's as if they ignited a fire within your heart. You smile and laugh more, look down at your feet to get relief from the intensity of your eyes meeting, and feel a rush of adrenaline. Suddenly, your problems seem to disappear, and your life is filled with the anticipation of love.

"Each date builds on the last. First it's candy and flowers, and then candlelight dinners for two in secluded restaurants, or walks on a deserted beach. The joy and excitement of getting to know each other is addictive. Your manners are impeccable as you show care and consideration for each other. Romance involves doing everything in one's power to please the other. Each wants the other to love them more than anyone else in the world. You love and you feel loved in a way that simply flows effortlessly.

"Some psychologists say that we all have about 70 hours worth of information to tell others about ourselves when we are in our twenties or thirties. During initial dating, we hang on each other's every word.

It's exciting, especially while discussing ideas, to discover that our date feels exactly like us. We announce to others that we have at last met our soul mate. We believe we have found our *one and only*, our *true love*. Life's future is colored with thoughts of perfection, harmony, and an eternal love affair with the new found love of our life."

Sarah sighed. "I remember those days."

"Me too," Jake added.

"During that time we are polite and courteous to each other. We would never dream of criticizing or causing hurt in any way. We resist negative thoughts first because of the love we feel, and second for fear of losing the other's love. We can talk about anything. Our soul mate will listen with intensity and an eager desire to get to know us better. We can express the deep feelings of our heart and our lover will express understanding. Empathy is the key word that describes our idyllic relationship."

"I have trouble practicing empathy," Jake continued. "It's so easy to forget how we started, and lapse into bad habits when there's so much going on in our lives."

"Somewhere along the way, with children, changing diapers, paying bills, painting the house, earning a living, or finishing school, the romance can get lost. The vicissitudes of life can be traumatic on a marriage. Lovers' talk is reduced to harsh words. Husbands exit from the front porch with a note of bitterness on their lips. Wives drop off their children at day care wondering why in the world they married such a cad.

"If we don't keep the romance alive, our mate may fall in love with someone else. Enough days filled with harsh words, and an all-too-convenient-colleague with a listening ear, can turn into a secret love affair at sunset.

"Remember the *Five Pillars of a Successful Celestial Marriage?* The third one in particular?"

Sarah perked up. "You bet. Number three is a weekly date with your spouse."

"That's right, Sarah. A date night is critical in this day and age when men and women have many opportunities to fall in love in the work place or during extracurricular activities. A weekly date with our spouse becomes just as important as Family Home Evening. There are many benefits to having a weekly date. What do you think they include?"

"Hey this is right up my alley. I can think of a couple. Ready?" Sarah began reeling them off.

◆ One continues the excitement of the courtship and eliminates the need to find love from another source.

◆ One feels special and not just a meal provider, maid, laundress, wage earner, repairman or taxi cab driver for the children.

◆ One has a chance to be alone with their true love, away from the vicissitudes of life.

◆ One can enjoy being the focus of attention from their spouse.

"That's great Sarah. And here are some more," I added.

◆ The partners are able to communicate with eyes, body language and other subtle yet important cues that are lost in the hectic schedule of day-to-day life with the family.

◆ Dating strengthens the love relationship.

◆ Dates can create new positive memories, rather than only looking back to the past longingly.

◆ Dating gives both spouses something to look forward to when the pressures of life are so demanding.

◆ A weekly date sets a wonderful example for your children. They will learn from your example, how to treat their future husband or wife.

◆ A weekly date says: Our marriage, my relationship with you, my love for you is my top priority in life.

"People are good at finding excuses for not going on dates with their spouse. I've divided them up into nine groups.

The 'Hated Dating' Group. These people didn't like dating in the first place and were so glad to have the so-called 'game playing' over with, they collapse into a world of Friday night TV and couch potato-itis. Once a month they might attend a temple night, potluck at church, or take the kids for miniature golf on the weekend. But, they never go with their wife or husband anywhere alone.

The 'Too Busy Volunteering' Group. These folks are constantly booked to the hilt, with no time left over for dating their spouse. Everything else takes priority, from community banquets, fundraisers, volunteer work at school for carnivals, rummage sales, to school basketball games. These are wonderful people and everybody's favorite volunteer worker because they will spend whatever time it takes accomplishing work for a cause, every cause except their marriage! They are addicted to benefits they receive from service, and appear to be noble and great. However, they ignore the most important person in their lives, their eternal soul mate.

The 'Scrooge' Group. These individuals insist that dating is expensive, and they cannot afford to waste money on dates. So, they avoid them completely. They squelch any suggestion a spouse might offer to spend time together inexpensively. Unfortunately, these people are uncreative and can't conceive of the many free options available such as: taking a walk together around a lovely lake, walking on the beach, having a picnic in a park, playing catch in the back yard, drawing up plans for a dream home, taking a shower or bath together when the kids are gone, car shopping without buying, playing board games at home, or just talking about each other's dreams. There are hundreds of free dates.

"Romance isn't just about getting out of the house for candlelit dinners for two. It is about keeping your relationship with your spouse your number one priority. It is showing by action, namely a weekly date, that 'I'd rather be with you than do anything else in the world. I'd rather experience life with you than anyone else in the world. I'd rather have adventures with you than anyone else in the world. I'd rather talk to you than anyone else in the world. I don't want to miss what you are thinking and feeling and doing. I can't wait to be alone with you.'

The 'Duty' Group. This group refuses to date because they have obligations like gardening or mowing the lawn. This group cancels Friday night dates to finish the laundry, can the pears, fix the plumbing, organize the food storage, or scrub the floor. This group just can't understand that the floor, plumbing, and laundry can wait until Saturday morning. Some will say, 'But I'm showing my spouse that I love them by keeping up the house or fixing the garage door opener.' Yes, this statement is true but not when it takes the place of a date over a period of weeks, then months, then years. At this point the husband becomes a handyman who happens to occupy the same house, and the wife becomes a mere housekeeper. What happened to the lovers? Trust me, one day they'll find love elsewhere.

The 'I'm Too Tired' Group. This group claims that weekends are the only time they have to come down from the pressures of work, and go to bed early. Usually, these people, who say that they're too tired to date, instead squander their time watching television or surfing the internet.

"The other night, Conrad and I had spent hours moving to another house. I was tired and ached all over. Conrad insisted that we stop and go out on our regular date. He had planned for us to go to a Thai restaurant for dinner. I didn't want to go. I was too tired. I guess I just wanted to *veg* out in front of the TV. Conrad persisted, so I agreed to go. I quickly changed clothes and hopped into the car. My mood gradually changed, and once we were at the restaurant, in an out-of-the-way booth, I was so happy to be on a date. We talked and talked and enjoyed each other. After a day of hard work, we were both filled with love from each other. It was a terrific example of the rewards that come from following the advice to date every week. Being 'too tired' is most often a matter of attitude. When we use it as an excuse, we are saying to our spouse, 'I don't love you enough to put out the energy to go out on a date.' Beware if you fall into this group. Your spouse will find someone who will have the energy!

The 'Children Come First' Group. These people insist that they have to attend all of their children's games or activities. Sometimes, especially with several children, that could mean an activity every weekend evening. Months could pass before an opportunity opens to schedule a date with a spouse. There is nothing wrong with supporting one's children, but not to the expense of never having a date together. Children will survive an occasional absence by the parents. Compromise will be understood by the children, especially when they witness the benefits that come from their parents' healthy relationship.

"My mother was a wonderful example of always putting my father first. I knew without a doubt that my mother loved my father, and I knew that he loved her. They showed it. When the children get their way and end up with the lion's share of a parent's time, children receive the wrong message. They not only become selfish, but they also do not learn to respect the union of marriage and all that it entails. Children need to see their parents dating. They need that wonderful example of love, and will learn a lesson that will help them immeasurably when they are married with children.

"There are some parents who don't date because they feel an obligation to their infant children. Some have the attitude that no one can baby-sit them. They don't trust anyone, and sometimes they just can't afford the luxury. One ward in Seattle solved this problem. The ward is full of young couples with babies. These couples formed a special group so they can trade babysitting. One couple will have Friday as their date night and another will take Saturday. Each in turn baby-sits the other couple's children on their respective date night. Trust and money are no longer a problem. Keeping a great relationship in a marriage is so important that creative solutions like this are essential.

The 'There's Nothing To Do' Group. This is a non-creative or at the very least, a lazy group. These people lack imagination. Instead of trying something new, they'll take the path of least resistance, turn on the TV, and zone out.

"Dating over the period of a long life requires imagination, innovation, and a willingness to try things that are new and different. One of my friends developed a unique idea for dating. They send their children over to a friend's house for the evening. They stay at home and read classic literature out loud together. They do the same thing almost every date. They read, discuss, and share. It's fun to talk to them because they always have interesting perspectives on life gained from their reading. Another couple spends their dates talking while they knit sweaters together. I really enjoy seeing them at church in their unusual sweaters. They were works of art, perfected on their dates. Another couple I knew took up the hobby of collecting antiques. Every Saturday, without the children, they would comb the countryside for antiques. They enjoy the history behind them, having many unusual adventures along the way. Another couple plays golf together, while they enjoy many hours of talk time.

"There is no excuse for the members of group seven since there are so many things to do in life with one's spouse.

The 'My Spouse Is Chronically Ill' Group. This group has many exceptions and must be handled carefully. Of course there are some situations in which a spouse is unable to date at all. There are temporary illnesses such as pneumonia, the flu, or even illnesses of longer duration that prevent dating. These are the exceptions. But what about the spouse who once had polio and is in a wheelchair for life? Can they date? Yes. In fact, the infirm or handicapped need to date perhaps more than anyone else. They need reassurance that they are loved and still attractive to the other person. Creativity is the key to dating in these situations. My Aunt Anna May is a wonderful example of this. She was stricken with polio when she was pregnant with her second son. She has spent most of her life in a wheelchair, but never lets her handicap prevent her from participating in life to the fullest. Several years after her husband died, she started dating. An old friend started taking her out. They did everything together. Eventually they were married. He wheels her chair around everywhere. They are still having a great time going on cruises and vacationing in exotic places. What an example they have been of true love and creative dating!

"Elizabeth Barrett Browning, a famous poet, suffered from a prolonged illness. However, during the time she was confined to her bed and home, she carried on a romance, writing some of her most profound love poems. We all need to feel loved. We all need romance no matter what condition we are in. When my second cousin's wife passed away, he was 90 years old. A year later he was very lonely. He needed love and romance. At 91 he married a 'young woman,' 76 years old!

"Elizabeth Barrett Browning demonstrated that romance can be carried out in the written word. A Friday night date with a sick husband or wife might entail reading them a story, holding their hand and telling them the story of how you fell in love with them. We never tire of hearing compliments and remembrances of our courtship. Dating an ill spouse shows true love. Sitting by his or her bedside and reading to your spouse shows total devotion and demonstrates profound love.

The 'You Never Want To Do What I Want To Do' Group. This group suffers from their lack of a willingness to sacrifice for their mate. (See chapter 6)

"A couple came to me for spiritual counseling. They had been married many years and were now both seventy years old. They claimed that they had nothing in common with each other. Their children were grown and had families of their own. The wife lived upstairs and the husband lived downstairs. When I asked them to live the Five Pillars of a Celestial Marriage, they groaned, glanced at each other and growled. With arms folded tightly in self-defense, a myriad of excuses tumbled from their lips like breaking rapids crashing down on the rocks. The wife complained that her husband never wanted to do anything that she wanted to do. The husband concurred. Neither one of them would even consider trying something that the other one might enjoy. The husband found it silly to think of dating each other at their age anyway. They were two stubborn individuals who refused to try something new.

"Another young couple I'll call Chandra and Jared, heard me tell the previous story in my Celestial Marriage class, and volunteered that they had the same problem. Neither one ever wanted to do anything the other one suggested. When I asked them how long they had been married, they confessed that they were newlyweds of a mere six months. This frightening confession was a step forward. They insisted that they didn't want to end up like the 70-year-old couple who lived on separate floors of their house!"

"What do couples like that do?" Sarah queried with genuine concern.

"Yeah. That's a horrid mess. Why did they get married in the first place?" Jake added.

"I can best answer that question by telling you another story from my marriage. Conrad was an avid racquetball player and was sure that

I would enjoy the sport too. He surprised me with a gift of a racquetball racket and special protective glasses. It was the promise of many wonderful dates together playing racquetball. I have to admit I can still feel the excitement I felt driving to the Olympic Health and Racquet Club for our first racquetball date. The racquet was short handled. I liked that feature. It was easy to swing in the air. I had never liked tennis because the racquet was too heavy and the handle too long for my slim ballet dancer's arm to swing in the air. Besides, the ball kept hitting my handle. A short handled racquet seemed like a great answer. Oh, and also, I really disliked running back and forth on a court just to hit a ball. Never having seen a racquetball game, I assumed you just stood in one area and took turns hitting the ball against a back wall. In the movie in my mind I could see it all. Conrad and I were dressed in Victorian clothes and playing a rather pleasant game of racquetball, a ladylike sport. My delusions were shattered the minute I set foot on the court, and Conrad began hitting the ball against the ceiling and side walls. 'Wait a minute,' I yelled out in emotional pain, trying to avoid getting hit by a wild ball zooming straight at my head. Conrad laughed and laughed. He couldn't believe that I had had such a gross misconception of the game. My dear friend Judy tried to help me learn to play racquetball during the next few months. But it was to no avail, because I just didn't like the game. Needless to say, my days of playing racquetball with my husband were numbered! Conrad was great about it. When I apologized all over the place for not enjoying the sport and feeling terrible that he had spent so much money on a brand new racquet for me, he simply said in an unconditionally loving voice, 'It's totally unimportant. There are so many other things we can enjoy together. Besides, Alexander and Elisabeth can use this racquet when they play racquetball with me.' He is not a member of the 'You never want to do anything that I want to do' group!

"Many spouses close their minds to their differences in taste, and give up trying when something they like does not fit with their spouse. They expend no effort to find other hobbies, sports, or activities that can be shared, settling for separation of interests, sewing the first seeds of future divorce. The spouses in this group who stop dating because they can't find common interests, send messages to their spouse: 1. You aren't worth the effort to find something to do together that we both enjoy, and 2. We have nothing in common and probably shouldn't have married in the first place. These couples are doomed to live a life together but separate, in quiet desperation, until someone else comes along to fulfill their needs.

"For example, the other day the Sunday School president called me to talk about the scheduling of my next Celestial Marriage class. As we talked, he told me the story of a boyhood friend whose parents had recently divorced. The friend's parents had been married in the temple and the husband had been a stake president for nine years. I asked if either had remarried. He said that the wife was engaged very soon after the divorce, and was the one who had asked for the divorce in the first place. Audaciously I said, 'I bet I know why they got a divorce.' 'You do?' he countered incredulously. 'Yes,' I continued. 'I bet that they didn't have a weekly date except to the temple or a stake or ward function. Or, they didn't have talk time because the stake president spent late hours in meetings or counseling people, so by the time he arrived home, his wife was already asleep. Since she is now engaged and there was no adultery involved, it says to me that she wasn't getting enough attention from her husband, and found someone who would listen to her and court her.' 'That makes perfect sense,' the Sunday School President affirmed.

"Talk time is when we learn each other's interests. If we don't spend that time, we lose opportunities to develop common goals and interests. It's critical so that we can avoid becoming a member of this group. Talk time is an extension of dating. It is the replacement for the phone calls between dates when a couple was courting. It is that daily dose of love that we all need. It is acknowledging that the other person's life is important to hear about daily.

"There are probably more groups of people who have excuses for not dating, but these are the primary ones to avoid. The point of all this is that romance is important in marriage, and dating is the mechanism we use to keep it alive. Dating is critical to marriage in many ways. It is important that through our dating, we have more positive experiences with each other than negative ones. We need to have good times to balance the heartaches that are inevitable from just being human.

"Life was meant to be joyful. In the *Book of Mormon* it says that this life is the time for us to have joy.[9] That means that our marriage is meant to be joyful, loving and happy. Dating keeps it that way.

"Romance is timeless, and the physical aspect of love is important. One time, my friend Monica's 11-year-old daughter asked her, 'You and Dad don't have sex, do you? You're too old, aren't you? And anyway, you're not going to have any more children.' This precious query was representative of her innocence. The fact is, physical expressions of love are a wonderful way of showing our mate just how much we love them. No matter how old we are, no matter how infirm, no matter how

9 Nephi 2:24 (*Book of Mormon*)

pregnant, we can still touch, or kiss and hug and show physical signs of love. Hugging and touching are wonderful ways to express romantic love.

"Some men, unfortunately, think that kissing and hugging are only a means to an end, which must always culminate in sex. Generally speaking, this kind of man never experienced seeing his own parents kissing and hugging around the home. Just as parents hug and kiss their children frequently in moments of praise and love, so too are hugs and kisses between spouses, independent of sex, important to keep a marriage flourishing.

"Many wives have complained to me, saying things such as, 'After marriage, my husband stopped holding my hand, hugging and cuddling me.' Unless they had sex, there wasn't any other expressions of physical love. Their husbands had eliminated all of the simple touching and kissing they had in courtship. Women and men both need the continuation of physical courtship, replete with hugs, kisses, and tender touches throughout the days, weeks, months and years of life together.

"It is important to hug and kiss each other as expressions of love without the follow-through of sex. It shows unconditional expression of love without expectation of returned favor. These signs can be given for no specific reason or for appreciation for a job well done, such as a great dinner, fixing a plugged toilet, taking out the garbage or cleaning out the attic. Holding hands is a must on dates. Hugging during a romantic dinner, or in a movie theatre, or when least expected, keeps the romance in marriage alive. These add to the romance of marriage and are necessary 'marriage insurance payments.' They insure you when real problems occur and you need to know that your spouse truly loves you.

"One of my friends told me that he never saw his parents hug, hold hands or kiss. How sad. He said that they had not learned how to give each other romantic love. I can still see my father kissing my mother every night when he came home from work. I loved seeing how much he loved her. Sometimes, he would sweep her up in his arms and spin her around in the air or dance around the kitchen with her for just a few moments. They'd laugh and kiss again, and mother would continue on with dinner while my father read the newspaper or prepared for a meeting at church. These were the special moments that helped them keep their romantic, celestial marriage alive.

"There are numerous books written on creative dating. They will give you ideas, but it really is up to you and your personal tastes. Just make sure that you give to each other the kind of dates the other one needs. Dating will strengthen your marriage, and ensure that you have romantic love. It's something we all need throughout the years, and will draw you closer romantically.

"You've been awfully quiet during the last fifteen minutes. Are you two asleep with your eyes open?" I queried. Jake and Sarah laughed.

Jake yawned dramatically. "We agree with what you're saying. Don't we honey?"

"Yup. What's there to understand? It's so straightforward. So, honey, what romantic date are you going to plan for us next Friday?"

This was my exit cue for the evening.

ASSIGNMENT NUMBER NINE

Have a weekly date with your spouse.

SUGGESTIONS FOR FREE OR
ALMOST FREE DATES TO GET YOU STARTED

1. Prepare an easy dinner together. Then go to a romantic spot and kiss and hug while you gaze at the stars.

2. Teach your mate a skill that you have such as playing the guitar, ballroom dancing, or throwing the shot put.

3. Learn a foreign language together and practice on each other on date night (tapes and books are available in the public library).

4. Talk a friend into dressing up in a crazy costume to present your mate with a homemade gift, a love poem that you authored, and an invitation to meet you at a local park to read a book together.

5. Send an invitation to your mate inviting him or her to a secret rendezvous with their secret lover–you! (Of course make sure there are obvious clues in the note so that they know it is you and not some kook!) Arrange for friends to take the children overnight with a promise to reciprocate. Transform your home into a bed and breakfast. Set the mood with plenty of candles. Make up a fruit basket and place it on the nightstand by your bed. Put mints on the pillows. Take an evening stroll under the stars to add to the mood of the evening. Have goblets and sparkling cider ready for a toast to your celestial marriage.

6. On a warm summer night, dress up in formal clothing, take along a portable CD player with your favorite dance music, find a deserted parking lot or other outdoor location, and dance under the stars (make sure you're not disturbing the neighborhood).
7. Read and discuss books together.
8. Cook together.
9. Learn a sport together during which you can talk and share.
10. If you both enjoy gardening, garden together while you talk.
11. Plan your dream house together.
12. Write a book together.
13. Go to a park and swing and ride the teeter-totter.
14. Walk around a nearby lake, river, or along the beach.
15. Take a picnic dinner in a basket, sit on a blanket, and watch a sunset.
16. Play in the snow together and a build a snowman.
17. Pretend that you are a specialist at a Health Spa. Stay in character acting out the part giving him or her a bath, shampoo, and manicure. Then the rest of the romantic night is up to you!
18. Pretend you are a Swedish Masseuse and give your husband or wife a body massage.
19. Comb the second hand shops to find yourself a military or policeman-like outfit, or doctor coat or whatever uniform your wife fancies. Then call for her wearing the suit one Friday date night as a surprise. Act out a complete night of fun. The reversal is fun too. The wife can meet her husband at the door wearing a traditional nurse's white uniform, etc.
20. Take your husband or wife shopping and watch them try on dozens of suits or dresses. Praise him or her and look at them as if seeing for the first time.
21. Go car shopping and dream.
22. Go to a museum together. Ask each other's opinion and genuinely be interested. Gain new insights on your partner's taste and views, whether it is an art museum, natural museum of history, science museum, etc. Many museums have a free day once a month.
23. Have a series of dates you call *international nights*. Plan and cook a foreign dinner together while also studying the country.
24. Attend a free sporting event and feast on homemade popcorn you bring along.
25. Go roller skating or ice-skating together (look for the free nights).

26. Take food out of your food storage, make several box loads complete with paper plates and a can opener. Drive the streets handing out care packages to the homeless on the streets saving one box load for yourselves. Then go to a park and eat the same meal you gave to the street people. Take turns counting your blessings and discussing the meaning of life.
27. Go to your husband's or wife's office and behind closed doors pretend like you are business associates flirting. You can start a secret affair with your spouse.
28. Read about another era together: World War II, Roaring Twenties, Hippie Sixties and Seventies, Civil War, Revolutionary War, the Knights of the Round Table, Roman Era etc. Choose appropriate names for each other from that era, make up a romantic problem and extemporaneously act out the mini drama.
29. Enjoy a free preview movie (they advertise them in the newspaper). Afterwards, drive to a beautiful location, park, eat homemade cookies and discuss the movie. In the summertime, many large cities have free plays, ballets and concerts in the park. Take advantage of these date opportunities and then take a walk for an hour after the performance to talk about the experience together.
30. Check out the book *Please Understand Me* by Kiersey and Bates from the library and take the personality tests together. Then discuss them and marvel at each other's differences.
31. Play board games together such as: *Monopoly, Scrabble, Life,* etc.
32. Learn to remodel together. (It must be a mutual passion, or it is definitely not a date!)
33. Take up a craft or skill together such as: knitting, sewing, building cedar wood boxes for potted plants, etc.
34. Have several dates taking the exercises on the following pages.

Remember This Key To Dating: The date must be something that both of you want to do! Be open to new ideas. You are creating memories.

Exercise #1: Romance for a Date Night

List all of the romantic dates and/or expressions of love that you want your spouse to do for you to keep the romantic love alive in your marriage. (Put a star by the ones that mean the most to you.)

1.

2.

3.

4.

5.

6.

7.

8.

9.

10.

EXERCISE #2: ROMANTIC LOVE,
KEEPING IT ALIVE IN YOUR MARRIAGE

List the things that made you fall in love with your spouse when you were courting: qualities he or she had, dates that were romantic, things that meant a lot to you.

1.

2.

3.

4.

5.

6.

7.

8.

9.

10.

Now make a goal of reviving those qualities and sharing them with your spouse.

What do you miss now in terms of romantic love that seems to be absent from your marriage?

MAKE A COMMITMENT TO REVIVE
ROMANTIC LOVE IN YOUR MARRIAGE

CHAPTER 10

THE PLATINUM RULE
OF MARRIAGE

The early summer winds were blowing through our hair. Our children were happily building sandcastles. Jake, Sarah and I were deep in thought. This was our final meeting. Today I would reveal Secret Number Ten for achieving a successful celestial marriage. I drank in a breath of fresh salt air, taking in the aroma of seaweed.

"Can you guess what secret number ten is?" I asked.

"I don't have a clue? Do you Jake?" Sarah answered.

Jake shook his head.

"When Moses received the revelation from the Lord on the Ten Commandments, it changed the Israelites' lives. They needed basic laws to govern themselves. They had been slaves. They had been punished for thinking original thoughts and worshipping their God. Some of them did not fully understand their religion and Abraham's covenant with God. The Ten Commandments were straightforward and needed little interpretation. It was God's way of helping these people. Such was also the case with the 'Golden Rule.' Christ taught this principle in his famous Sermon on the Mount. In Matthew 7:12, it says 'Therefore all things whatsoever ye would that men should do to you, do ye even so to them: for this is the law and the prophets.' The idea was to teach the people that they should be kind to their neighbor if they expected kindness in return. They should help each other if they wanted others to help them. And so it continues. This 'Golden Rule' is often talked about by people who do not affiliate themselves with any religion. It is a universal principle accepted by the general populace and is paraphrased in many forms."

"The Golden Rule is the last secret?" Jake asked.

"Not quite. But a good guess. In a celestial marriage we are striving to reach a perfect oneness with our spouse. In order to do this, there is yet a higher law than the Golden Rule in marriage and it is called: *The Platinum Rule.*

"It goes like this: *Do unto your spouse as they want you to do unto them.*

"I'm not sure I get it? How is that different?" Sarah interjected.

"Okay, here's an example. Husband George loves to have his back rubbed but hates to have it scratched. Wife Roberta, on the other hand, loves to have her back scratched but hates to have it rubbed. If the couple followed the Golden Rule, George would be rubbing his wife's back and Roberta would be scratching George's back. Both would be miserable. If, however, they practiced the *Platinum Rule of Marriage*, George would be scratching his wife's back and Roberta would be rubbing George's back. Both of them would feel loved because they were receiving exactly what they both wanted."

"Okay. I'm beginning to get it. Please give us more examples."

"One of my friends was telling me about her birthday celebration. She had asked her husband to make her strawberry shortcake. Pete was happy to oblige. However, he made a fatal error. He made the strawberry shortcake the way he liked it, with sliced strawberries soaking in sugar for hours creating a large quantity of juice. By the time he served the dessert, the cake was soggy. Karen was upset. First of all, she hated strawberries swimming in sugar, and secondly, she didn't like a mushy, soaked cake underneath the strawberries. Pete had not followed the *Platinum Rule of Marriage*. The following week he repeated Karen's special birthday dinner complete with strawberry shortcake, but this time it was the way she liked it. As Karen bit into a piece of dry cake with sliced strawberries on top just barely sprinkled with sugar, she was happy and felt truly loved. Pete had successfully made up for the first failure. The second dinner is an example of living the *Platinum Rule of Marriage*.

"This episode may sound trivial. One could argue that Karen should have been grateful that he made dinner for her at all. While that may be true, what we are talking about here is on a higher level. If we want to obtain a celestial marriage, we must give our spouse the kind of love that he or she wants and needs.

"It sounds like a simple principle, but many couples have problems with it. I have talked to many people who have been telling their spouse what they prefer for years, and have had their request repeatedly ignored. Whether it is a husband who continues to grab at his wife when she's on the phone, or a wife who continues to make scrambled eggs for breakfast when she knows her husband doesn't like them, both can be important issues in a marriage. When a spouse refuses to respond to a polite request regarding preferences, it hurts the marriage tremendously. This action sends a message to our spouse that we no longer care if we please them. Subconsciously, it authors a profound statement to our spouse: 'I don't love you as much as I did when we were courting, and frankly, I don't care if I please you anymore.'"

"I understand totally," Sarah responded. "I think that is a problem we sometimes have. Jake does things for me that he would like, even if I don't like them. And I admit I do the same to him sometimes."

"If we truly love our spouse, we would never do anything to them that they don't like. If we're communicating on a regular basis with talk time, we'll know what those things are, and avoid them. Remember when you were courting, you tried to do everything right to please your date? If your date didn't like something, you didn't do it. That is what celestial marriage is all about: giving your spouse the kind of love that they want. It means remembering that they don't like scrambled eggs for breakfast even if you do. It means not grabbing at them when they are on the phone or other inappropriate times, because they don't like it. It means focusing on your mate's needs, and doing everything in your power to give him or her the kind of love he or she wants.

"When my husband and I were courting, he would hold my hand in a movie theatre and rub the center of my palm with his thumb. I didn't like it, but I didn't want to make an issue of it. I thought to myself, 'I know he loves me and doesn't know how to give me the kind of affection that I would like. How could he possibly know that I wouldn't like my palm being rubbed at this point in our relationship? No doubt this kind of affection is probably what he would like.' He was practicing the Golden Rule. So, I started to rub his palm with my thumb. He loved it. At that point in our relationship, all he knew was to give me the kind of love that he wanted. Turning around his gesture and realizing that's what he wanted, I felt was inspiration from the Lord. After the movie, I was able to tell him that I didn't like hand rubbing. I preferred firm hand holding. We laughed and felt closer together than ever. We had both learned a magical key, the beginning of our understanding of the *Platinum Rule*, in giving each other a true expression of our love in a way that it would be received as such.

"When I was co-writing a script with a colleague, we often had conversations about our families to flesh out characters. One day we were trying to understand and develop the heroine. In an effort to help the work along, my partner brought up an example. When he and his wife were first married, he inadvertently ripped off a piece of dangling thread from his suit coat and tossed it on the bedroom carpet by the closet. That night when he returned home from work, his wife was cold and sullen. He quizzed her, 'What's wrong honey?' She stonewalled, 'Nothing.' After a few unsuccessful interchanges, she volunteered that she was upset because he had dropped a thread on the carpet. He couldn't believe that such a little thing had been so catastrophic to her.

"I have to admit that when I first heard this story, I laughed to myself, thinking, 'My goodness! Most women are lucky if their husbands even hang up their clothes in the closet. Who cares about a thread?' However, over the years I have never forgotten 'The Thread Story,' because I realized that the thread symbolized this man's love for his wife. To feel loved, she needed him to show his love to her by respecting all of the work she did during the day cleaning the house. Dropping the thread on the floor meant that he didn't care if she had to vacuum all over again. You must understand that this woman was a white glove housekeeper. She couldn't go to bed at night unless everything was in perfect order, with hospital cleanliness in each room of the house. So, when her husband dropped the thread on the rug, she thought that he was saying, with his action, that he didn't love her. You better believe he never made that mistake again! All ripped threads were deposited in the nearest garbage receptacle. He learned the *Platinum Rule* that day. He learned that picking up the thread was a way of giving his wife the kind of love she wanted, fulfilling her wishes. It was a way of showing how much he loved her in the way in which she wanted to be loved.

"'Love is in the eye of the beholder.' We have all heard that expression regarding sex appeal and beauty. The same is true in how we feel loved by our mates. It is in the eye of the beholder, or shall we say, it is felt in the heart of the one being loved. I have often wished that I could enter a person's name into a computer, and print out a form that would tell me what they liked and didn't like.

"Sometimes I like to hug people as a gesture of love. It's a way of being happy for them when they tell me good news. Or, it's a way of congratulating them for a success in their lives, a prayer being answered, or a child getting an 'A' on a report card.

"One day, one of my girlfriends told me that she didn't like to be hugged by other women. To her it was insincere. She had experienced betrayal from old girlfriends, who showed love to her face with hugs, and then later hurt her by divulging confidential conversations. So, I learned to show love to her in the way she wanted, which was to listen, encourage, and keep her confidences. This gave her the understanding and unconditional love that she so desperately wanted from a girlfriend. I felt blessed that she told me how she felt so that I could learn to love her in the way she wanted, without hugs.

"Our spouse should not be a mystery. Our communication should be so open that we know what they like and dislike, and how they want to be loved. It is our job to remember these things. If we don't, we send a message loud and clear that we don't really care about our spouse. We are saying that we only care about ourselves and our wants and likes, and giving them an even stronger message that we don't love them enough to change.

"A woman who had trouble in her intimate relationship with her husband came to me for help. No matter how many times she told her spouse that she didn't like a particular behavior, night after night he would repeat it all over again. When she would politely ask him why he kept doing that to her when she didn't like it and had told him emphatically that she didn't like it, he would counter, 'I do it because I like it.' Over the years, their intimate relationship deteriorated because he wasn't willing to give her the kind of love she wanted. He only cared about his own pleasure. His selfishness finally drove a wedge between them. If only he had responded to her plea, they could have developed a physical oneness that is so crucial in a marriage.

"Another time, a young man taking my marriage class took me aside to tell me his problem. He didn't know what to do. He said that his wife refused to have intimate relations with him except once every two months. He was going crazy. He just couldn't take it. I asked him this question: 'Do you give her pleasure each and every time that you are intimate? Is she fulfilled?' He looked down at the floor. I said, 'No wonder. Get a few books from the library and open the doors of communication so that you can learn how to give her pleasure? Give her the kind of love that she needs. The result will be that you will have your needs fulfilled too.'

"Often the problems we inflict on each other can be summed up in our failure to live the *Platinum Rule of Marriage*. At all times, we must seek to give our spouse the kind of love that they want and need."

"That's it?" Jake asked incredulously.

"That's it," I continued.

"*We must love our spouse in the way in which they need and want to be loved.*

"I have a strong testimony of the importance of giving our mates the kind of love that they need. Therein lies true love. It is the pathway to a bond between partners that will endure for all eternity."

Sarah and Jake looked at me with pensive eyes.

"I know that if you live all ten of the secrets for achieving a successful celestial marriage, you will reach a oneness in your marriage attained by few in this life."

Sarah and I hugged, and Jake shook my hand goodbye.

"God bless you two. I know you can do it. You will achieve a successful celestial marriage."

They smiled at me gratefully and then hugged each other in a meaningful embrace.

The setting sun cast a long shadow of their two silhouettes. I grasped little Elisabeth's delicate hand and we started down the sandy beach towards home. I said a silent prayer, asking the Lord to bless them on their journey to a celestial marriage. As the sun set on the great Puget Sound, Elisabeth looked up at me and asked: "Are they going to be okay, Mommy?" I answered "They're going to be just fine."

ASSIGNMENT NUMBER TEN:

Live the "Platinum Rule of Marriage:"

Exercise:

1. Each spouse lists ways in which he or she wants to be loved.
2. Trade lists, and write down the differences between each other.
3. Memorize how your spouse wants love and commit to love them in these ways.
4. Discuss how you have shown love to your spouse in ways they don't like. Make a commitment to stop doing these things.
5. Repeat to your spouse how you will now show them love.

MAKE A COMMITMENT TO LOVE YOUR SPOUSE IN A WAY THAT HE OR SHE WANTS.

Remember: Actions always speak louder than words.

ACKNOWLEDGEMENTS

Special thanks to Dr. Lynn Flowers, for his invaluable assistance. He spent many hours editing my book out of love and kindness. I am deeply grateful to him for his support and confidence in my project.

Thanks to my friends: Holly Metcalf, Judith and Troy Williams, and Judy Roloson for their suggestions and support; and to Russ Nickel for researching some of the quotes.

I am grateful to Creede and Sharleen Lambard for adding their professional touches to my book.